C-4055   CAREER EXAMINATION SERIES

*This is your
PASSBOOK for...*

Certified Professional Coder (CPC)

*Test Preparation Study Guide
Questions & Answers*

NATIONAL LEARNING CORPORATION®

COPYRIGHT NOTICE

This book is SOLELY intended for, is sold ONLY to, and its use is RESTRICTED to individual, bona fide applicants or candidates who qualify by virtue of having seriously filed applications for appropriate license, certificate, professional and/or promotional advancement, higher school matriculation, scholarship, or other legitimate requirements of education and/or governmental authorities.

This book is NOT intended for use, class instruction, tutoring, training, duplication, copying, reprinting, excerption, or adaptation, etc., by:

1) Other publishers
2) Proprietors and/or Instructors of "Coaching" and/or Preparatory Courses
3) Personnel and/or Training Divisions of commercial, industrial, and governmental organizations
4) Schools, colleges, or universities and/or their departments and staffs, including teachers and other personnel
5) Testing Agencies or Bureaus
6) Study groups which seek by the purchase of a single volume to copy and/or duplicate and/or adapt this material for use by the group as a whole without having purchased individual volumes for each of the members of the group
7) Et al.

Such persons would be in violation of appropriate Federal and State statutes.

PROVISION OF LICENSING AGREEMENTS – Recognized educational, commercial, industrial, and governmental institutions and organizations, and others legitimately engaged in educational pursuits, including training, testing, and measurement activities, may address request for a licensing agreement to the copyright owners, who will determine whether, and under what conditions, including fees and charges, the materials in this book may be used them. In other words, a licensing facility exists for the legitimate use of the material in this book on other than an individual basis. However, it is asseverated and affirmed here that the material in this book CANNOT be used without the receipt of the express permission of such a licensing agreement from the Publishers. Inquiries re licensing should be addressed to the company, attention rights and permissions department.

All rights reserved, including the right of reproduction in whole or in part, in any form or by any means, electronic or mechanical, including photocopying, recording, or by any information storage and retrieval system, without permission in writing from the Publisher.

Copyright © 2025 by
National Learning Corporation

212 Michael Drive, Syosset, NY 11791
(516) 921-8888 • www.passbooks.com
E-mail: info@passbooks.com

PASSBOOK® SERIES

THE *PASSBOOK® SERIES* has been created to prepare applicants and candidates for the ultimate academic battlefield – the examination room.

At some time in our lives, each and every one of us may be required to take an examination – for validation, matriculation, admission, qualification, registration, certification, or licensure.

Based on the assumption that every applicant or candidate has met the basic formal educational standards, has taken the required number of courses, and read the necessary texts, the *PASSBOOK® SERIES* furnishes the one special preparation which may assure passing with confidence, instead of failing with insecurity. Examination questions – together with answers – are furnished as the basic vehicle for study so that the mysteries of the examination and its compounding difficulties may be eliminated or diminished by a sure method.

This book is meant to help you pass your examination provided that you qualify and are serious in your objective.

The entire field is reviewed through the huge store of content information which is succinctly presented through a provocative and challenging approach – the question-and-answer method.

A climate of success is established by furnishing the correct answers at the end of each test.

You soon learn to recognize types of questions, forms of questions, and patterns of questioning. You may even begin to anticipate expected outcomes.

You perceive that many questions are repeated or adapted so that you can gain acute insights, which may enable you to score many sure points.

You learn how to confront new questions, or types of questions, and to attack them confidently and work out the correct answers.

You note objectives and emphases, and recognize pitfalls and dangers, so that you may make positive educational adjustments.

Moreover, you are kept fully informed in relation to new concepts, methods, practices, and directions in the field.

You discover that you are actually taking the examination all the time: you are preparing for the examination by "taking" an examination, not by reading extraneous and/or supererogatory textbooks.

In short, this PASSBOOK®, used directedly, should be an important factor in helping you to pass your test.

CERTIFIED PROFESSIONAL CODER (CPC)

DUTIES

As a Certified Professional Coder (CPC), you are responsible for the accurate assignment of codes to diagnoses and procedures in order to insure proper financial reimbursement from insurance companies and government agencies. Certified coders use a universally recognized coding system and must insure correct code selection for compliance with federal regulations and insurance requirements. This information is used to prepare statistical reports made available to private clinics and for public health concerns.

SCOPE OF THE EXAMINATION

The <u>written test</u> will cover knowledge, skills and/or abilities in such areas as:

1. Coding and compliance;
2. Medical and anatomical terminology;
3. Evaluation and management;
4. Radiology, pathology and medicine; and
5. Surgical and anesthesia coding.

HOW TO TAKE A TEST

I. YOU MUST PASS AN EXAMINATION

A. *WHAT EVERY CANDIDATE SHOULD KNOW*

Examination applicants often ask us for help in preparing for the written test. What can I study in advance? What kinds of questions will be asked? How will the test be given? How will the papers be graded?

As an applicant for a civil service examination, you may be wondering about some of these things. Our purpose here is to suggest effective methods of advance study and to describe civil service examinations.

Your chances for success on this examination can be increased if you know how to prepare. Those "pre-examination jitters" can be reduced if you know what to expect. You can even experience an adventure in good citizenship if you know why civil service exams are given.

B. *WHY ARE CIVIL SERVICE EXAMINATIONS GIVEN?*

Civil service examinations are important to you in two ways. As a citizen, you want public jobs filled by employees who know how to do their work. As a job seeker, you want a fair chance to compete for that job on an equal footing with other candidates. The best-known means of accomplishing this two-fold goal is the competitive examination.

Exams are widely publicized throughout the nation. They may be administered for jobs in federal, state, city, municipal, town or village governments or agencies.

Any citizen may apply, with some limitations, such as the age or residence of applicants. Your experience and education may be reviewed to see whether you meet the requirements for the particular examination. When these requirements exist, they are reasonable and applied consistently to all applicants. Thus, a competitive examination may cause you some uneasiness now, but it is your privilege and safeguard.

C. *HOW ARE CIVIL SERVICE EXAMS DEVELOPED?*

Examinations are carefully written by trained technicians who are specialists in the field known as "psychological measurement," in consultation with recognized authorities in the field of work that the test will cover. These experts recommend the subject matter areas or skills to be tested; only those knowledges or skills important to your success on the job are included. The most reliable books and source materials available are used as references. Together, the experts and technicians judge the difficulty level of the questions.

Test technicians know how to phrase questions so that the problem is clearly stated. Their ethics do not permit "trick" or "catch" questions. Questions may have been tried out on sample groups, or subjected to statistical analysis, to determine their usefulness.

Written tests are often used in combination with performance tests, ratings of training and experience, and oral interviews. All of these measures combine to form the best-known means of finding the right person for the right job.

II. HOW TO PASS THE WRITTEN TEST

A. NATURE OF THE EXAMINATION

To prepare intelligently for civil service examinations, you should know how they differ from school examinations you have taken. In school you were assigned certain definite pages to read or subjects to cover. The examination questions were quite detailed and usually emphasized memory. Civil service exams, on the other hand, try to discover your present ability to perform the duties of a position, plus your potentiality to learn these duties. In other words, a civil service exam attempts to predict how successful you will be. Questions cover such a broad area that they cannot be as minute and detailed as school exam questions.

In the public service similar kinds of work, or positions, are grouped together in one "class." This process is known as *position-classification*. All the positions in a class are paid according to the salary range for that class. One class title covers all of these positions, and they are all tested by the same examination.

B. FOUR BASIC STEPS

1) Study the announcement

How, then, can you know what subjects to study? Our best answer is: "Learn as much as possible about the class of positions for which you've applied." The exam will test the knowledge, skills and abilities needed to do the work.

Your most valuable source of information about the position you want is the official exam announcement. This announcement lists the training and experience qualifications. Check these standards and apply only if you come reasonably close to meeting them.

The brief description of the position in the examination announcement offers some clues to the subjects which will be tested. Think about the job itself. Review the duties in your mind. Can you perform them, or are there some in which you are rusty? Fill in the blank spots in your preparation.

Many jurisdictions preview the written test in the exam announcement by including a section called "Knowledge and Abilities Required," "Scope of the Examination," or some similar heading. Here you will find out specifically what fields will be tested.

2) Review your own background

Once you learn in general what the position is all about, and what you need to know to do the work, ask yourself which subjects you already know fairly well and which need improvement. You may wonder whether to concentrate on improving your strong areas or on building some background in your fields of weakness. When the announcement has specified "some knowledge" or "considerable knowledge," or has used adjectives like "beginning principles of..." or "advanced ... methods," you can get a clue as to the number and difficulty of questions to be asked in any given field. More questions, and hence broader coverage, would be included for those subjects which are more important in the work. Now weigh your strengths and weaknesses against the job requirements and prepare accordingly.

3) Determine the level of the position

Another way to tell how intensively you should prepare is to understand the level of the job for which you are applying. Is it the entering level? In other words, is this the position in which beginners in a field of work are hired? Or is it an intermediate or advanced level? Sometimes this is indicated by such words as "Junior" or "Senior" in the class title. Other jurisdictions use Roman numerals to designate the level – Clerk I, Clerk II, for example. The word "Supervisor" sometimes appears in the title. If the level is not indicated by the title, check the description of duties. Will you be working under very close supervision, or will you have responsibility for independent decisions in this work?

4) Choose appropriate study materials

Now that you know the subjects to be examined and the relative amount of each subject to be covered, you can choose suitable study materials. For beginning level jobs, or even advanced ones, if you have a pronounced weakness in some aspect of your training, read a modern, standard textbook in that field. Be sure it is up to date and has general coverage. Such books are normally available at your library, and the librarian will be glad to help you locate one. For entry-level positions, questions of appropriate difficulty are chosen – neither highly advanced questions, nor those too simple. Such questions require careful thought but not advanced training.

If the position for which you are applying is technical or advanced, you will read more advanced, specialized material. If you are already familiar with the basic principles of your field, elementary textbooks would waste your time. Concentrate on advanced textbooks and technical periodicals. Think through the concepts and review difficult problems in your field.

These are all general sources. You can get more ideas on your own initiative, following these leads. For example, training manuals and publications of the government agency which employs workers in your field can be useful, particularly for technical and professional positions. A letter or visit to the government department involved may result in more specific study suggestions, and certainly will provide you with a more definite idea of the exact nature of the position you are seeking.

III. KINDS OF TESTS

Tests are used for purposes other than measuring knowledge and ability to perform specified duties. For some positions, it is equally important to test ability to make adjustments to new situations or to profit from training. In others, basic mental abilities not dependent on information are essential. Questions which test these things may not appear as pertinent to the duties of the position as those which test for knowledge and information. Yet they are often highly important parts of a fair examination. For very general questions, it is almost impossible to help you direct your study efforts. What we can do is to point out some of the more common of these general abilities needed in public service positions and describe some typical questions.

1) General information

Broad, general information has been found useful for predicting job success in some kinds of work. This is tested in a variety of ways, from vocabulary lists to questions about current events. Basic background in some field of work, such as sociology or economics, may be sampled in a group of questions. Often these are principles which have become familiar to most persons through exposure rather than through formal training. It is difficult to advise you how to study for these questions; being alert to the world around you is our best suggestion.

2) Verbal ability

An example of an ability needed in many positions is verbal or language ability. Verbal ability is, in brief, the ability to use and understand words. Vocabulary and grammar tests are typical measures of this ability. Reading comprehension or paragraph interpretation questions are common in many kinds of civil service tests. You are given a paragraph of written material and asked to find its central meaning.

3) Numerical ability

Number skills can be tested by the familiar arithmetic problem, by checking paired lists of numbers to see which are alike and which are different, or by interpreting charts and graphs. In the latter test, a graph may be printed in the test booklet which you are asked to use as the basis for answering questions.

4) Observation

A popular test for law-enforcement positions is the observation test. A picture is shown to you for several minutes, then taken away. Questions about the picture test your ability to observe both details and larger elements.

5) Following directions

In many positions in the public service, the employee must be able to carry out written instructions dependably and accurately. You may be given a chart with several columns, each column listing a variety of information. The questions require you to carry out directions involving the information given in the chart.

6) Skills and aptitudes

Performance tests effectively measure some manual skills and aptitudes. When the skill is one in which you are trained, such as typing or shorthand, you can practice. These tests are often very much like those given in business school or high school courses. For many of the other skills and aptitudes, however, no short-time preparation can be made. Skills and abilities natural to you or that you have developed throughout your lifetime are being tested.

Many of the general questions just described provide all the data needed to answer the questions and ask you to use your reasoning ability to find the answers. Your best preparation for these tests, as well as for tests of facts and ideas, is to be at your physical and mental best. You, no doubt, have your own methods of getting into an exam-taking mood and keeping "in shape." The next section lists some ideas on this subject.

IV. KINDS OF QUESTIONS

Only rarely is the "essay" question, which you answer in narrative form, used in civil service tests. Civil service tests are usually of the short-answer type. Full instructions for answering these questions will be given to you at the examination. But in case this is your first experience with short-answer questions and separate answer sheets, here is what you need to know:

1) Multiple-choice Questions

Most popular of the short-answer questions is the "multiple choice" or "best answer" question. It can be used, for example, to test for factual knowledge, ability to solve problems or judgment in meeting situations found at work.

A multiple-choice question is normally one of three types—
- It can begin with an incomplete statement followed by several possible endings. You are to find the one ending which *best* completes the statement, although some of the others may not be entirely wrong.
- It can also be a complete statement in the form of a question which is answered by choosing one of the statements listed.

- It can be in the form of a problem – again you select the best answer.

Here is an example of a multiple-choice question with a discussion which should give you some clues as to the method for choosing the right answer:

When an employee has a complaint about his assignment, the action which will *best* help him overcome his difficulty is to
- A. discuss his difficulty with his coworkers
- B. take the problem to the head of the organization
- C. take the problem to the person who gave him the assignment
- D. say nothing to anyone about his complaint

In answering this question, you should study each of the choices to find which is best. Consider choice "A" – Certainly an employee may discuss his complaint with fellow employees, but no change or improvement can result, and the complaint remains unresolved. Choice "B" is a poor choice since the head of the organization probably does not know what assignment you have been given, and taking your problem to him is known as "going over the head" of the supervisor. The supervisor, or person who made the assignment, is the person who can clarify it or correct any injustice. Choice "C" is, therefore, correct. To say nothing, as in choice "D," is unwise. Supervisors have and interest in knowing the problems employees are facing, and the employee is seeking a solution to his problem.

2) True/False Questions

The "true/false" or "right/wrong" form of question is sometimes used. Here a complete statement is given. Your job is to decide whether the statement is right or wrong.

SAMPLE: A roaming cell-phone call to a nearby city costs less than a non-roaming call to a distant city.

This statement is wrong, or false, since roaming calls are more expensive.

This is not a complete list of all possible question forms, although most of the others are variations of these common types. You will always get complete directions for answering questions. Be sure you understand *how* to mark your answers – ask questions until you do.

V. RECORDING YOUR ANSWERS

Computer terminals are used more and more today for many different kinds of exams.

For an examination with very few applicants, you may be told to record your answers in the test booklet itself. Separate answer sheets are much more common. If this separate answer sheet is to be scored by machine – and this is often the case – it is highly important that you mark your answers correctly in order to get credit.

An electronic scoring machine is often used in civil service offices because of the speed with which papers can be scored. Machine-scored answer sheets must be marked with a pencil, which will be given to you. This pencil has a high graphite content which responds to the electronic scoring machine. As a matter of fact, stray dots may register as answers, so do not let your pencil rest on the answer sheet while you are pondering the correct answer. Also, if your pencil lead breaks or is otherwise defective, ask for another.

Since the answer sheet will be dropped in a slot in the scoring machine, be careful not to bend the corners or get the paper crumpled.

The answer sheet normally has five vertical columns of numbers, with 30 numbers to a column. These numbers correspond to the question numbers in your test booklet. After each number, going across the page are four or five pairs of dotted lines. These short dotted lines have small letters or numbers above them. The first two pairs may also have a "T" or "F" above the letters. This indicates that the first two pairs only are to be used if the questions are of the true-false type. If the questions are multiple choice, disregard the "T" and "F" and pay attention only to the small letters or numbers.

Answer your questions in the manner of the sample that follows:

32. The largest city in the United States is
    A. Washington, D.C.
    B. New York City
    C. Chicago
    D. Detroit
    E. San Francisco

1) Choose the answer you think is best. (New York City is the largest, so "B" is correct.)
2) Find the row of dotted lines numbered the same as the question you are answering. (Find row number 32)
3) Find the pair of dotted lines corresponding to the answer. (Find the pair of lines under the mark "B.")
4) Make a solid black mark between the dotted lines.

VI. BEFORE THE TEST

Common sense will help you find procedures to follow to get ready for an examination. Too many of us, however, overlook these sensible measures. Indeed, nervousness and fatigue have been found to be the most serious reasons why applicants fail to do their best on civil service tests. Here is a list of reminders:

- Begin your preparation early – Don't wait until the last minute to go scurrying around for books and materials or to find out what the position is all about.
- Prepare continuously – An hour a night for a week is better than an all-night cram session. This has been definitely established. What is more, a night a week for a month will return better dividends than crowding your study into a shorter period of time.
- Locate the place of the exam – You have been sent a notice telling you when and where to report for the examination. If the location is in a different town or otherwise unfamiliar to you, it would be well to inquire the best route and learn something about the building.
- Relax the night before the test – Allow your mind to rest. Do not study at all that night. Plan some mild recreation or diversion; then go to bed early and get a good night's sleep.
- Get up early enough to make a leisurely trip to the place for the test – This way unforeseen events, traffic snarls, unfamiliar buildings, etc. will not upset you.
- Dress comfortably – A written test is not a fashion show. You will be known by number and not by name, so wear something comfortable.

- Leave excess paraphernalia at home – Shopping bags and odd bundles will get in your way. You need bring only the items mentioned in the official notice you received; usually everything you need is provided. Do not bring reference books to the exam. They will only confuse those last minutes and be taken away from you when in the test room.
- Arrive somewhat ahead of time – If because of transportation schedules you must get there very early, bring a newspaper or magazine to take your mind off yourself while waiting.
- Locate the examination room – When you have found the proper room, you will be directed to the seat or part of the room where you will sit. Sometimes you are given a sheet of instructions to read while you are waiting. Do not fill out any forms until you are told to do so; just read them and be prepared.
- Relax and prepare to listen to the instructions
- If you have any physical problem that may keep you from doing your best, be sure to tell the test administrator. If you are sick or in poor health, you really cannot do your best on the exam. You can come back and take the test some other time.

VII. AT THE TEST

The day of the test is here and you have the test booklet in your hand. The temptation to get going is very strong. Caution! There is more to success than knowing the right answers. You must know how to identify your papers and understand variations in the type of short-answer question used in this particular examination. Follow these suggestions for maximum results from your efforts:

1) Cooperate with the monitor

The test administrator has a duty to create a situation in which you can be as much at ease as possible. He will give instructions, tell you when to begin, check to see that you are marking your answer sheet correctly, and so on. He is not there to guard you, although he will see that your competitors do not take unfair advantage. He wants to help you do your best.

2) Listen to all instructions

Don't jump the gun! Wait until you understand all directions. In most civil service tests you get more time than you need to answer the questions. So don't be in a hurry. Read each word of instructions until you clearly understand the meaning. Study the examples, listen to all announcements and follow directions. Ask questions if you do not understand what to do.

3) Identify your papers

Civil service exams are usually identified by number only. You will be assigned a number; you must not put your name on your test papers. Be sure to copy your number correctly. Since more than one exam may be given, copy your exact examination title.

4) Plan your time

Unless you are told that a test is a "speed" or "rate of work" test, speed itself is usually not important. Time enough to answer all the questions will be provided, but this does not mean that you have all day. An overall time limit has been set. Divide the total time (in minutes) by the number of questions to determine the approximate time you have for each question.

5) Do not linger over difficult questions

If you come across a difficult question, mark it with a paper clip (useful to have along) and come back to it when you have been through the booklet. One caution if you do this – be sure to skip a number on your answer sheet as well. Check often to be sure that you have not lost your place and that you are marking in the row numbered the same as the question you are answering.

6) Read the questions

Be sure you know what the question asks! Many capable people are unsuccessful because they failed to *read* the questions correctly.

7) Answer all questions

Unless you have been instructed that a penalty will be deducted for incorrect answers, it is better to guess than to omit a question.

8) Speed tests

It is often better NOT to guess on speed tests. It has been found that on timed tests people are tempted to spend the last few seconds before time is called in marking answers at random – without even reading them – in the hope of picking up a few extra points. To discourage this practice, the instructions may warn you that your score will be "corrected" for guessing. That is, a penalty will be applied. The incorrect answers will be deducted from the correct ones, or some other penalty formula will be used.

9) Review your answers

If you finish before time is called, go back to the questions you guessed or omitted to give them further thought. Review other answers if you have time.

10) Return your test materials

If you are ready to leave before others have finished or time is called, take ALL your materials to the monitor and leave quietly. Never take any test material with you. The monitor can discover whose papers are not complete, and taking a test booklet may be grounds for disqualification.

VIII. EXAMINATION TECHNIQUES

1) Read the general instructions carefully. These are usually printed on the first page of the exam booklet. As a rule, these instructions refer to the timing of the examination; the fact that you should not start work until the signal and must stop work at a signal, etc. If there are any *special* instructions, such as a choice of questions to be answered, make sure that you note this instruction carefully.

2) When you are ready to start work on the examination, that is as soon as the signal has been given, read the instructions to each question booklet, underline any key words or phrases, such as *least, best, outline, describe* and the like. In this way you will tend to answer as requested rather than discover on reviewing your paper that you *listed without describing*, that you selected the *worst* choice rather than the *best* choice, etc.

3) If the examination is of the objective or multiple-choice type – that is, each question will also give a series of possible answers: A, B, C or D, and you are called upon to select the best answer and write the letter next to that answer on your answer paper – it is advisable to start answering each question in turn. There may be anywhere from 50 to 100 such questions in the three or four hours allotted and you can see how much time would be taken if you read through all the questions before beginning to answer any. Furthermore, if you come across a question or group of questions which you know would be difficult to answer, it would undoubtedly affect your handling of all the other questions.

4) If the examination is of the essay type and contains but a few questions, it is a moot point as to whether you should read all the questions before starting to answer any one. Of course, if you are given a choice – say five out of seven and the like – then it is essential to read all the questions so you can eliminate the two that are most difficult. If, however, you are asked to answer all the questions, there may be danger in trying to answer the easiest one first because you may find that you will spend too much time on it. The best technique is to answer the first question, then proceed to the second, etc.

5) Time your answers. Before the exam begins, write down the time it started, then add the time allowed for the examination and write down the time it must be completed, then divide the time available somewhat as follows:
    - If 3-1/2 hours are allowed, that would be 210 minutes. If you have 80 objective-type questions, that would be an average of 2-1/2 minutes per question. Allow yourself no more than 2 minutes per question, or a total of 160 minutes, which will permit about 50 minutes to review.
    - If for the time allotment of 210 minutes there are 7 essay questions to answer, that would average about 30 minutes a question. Give yourself only 25 minutes per question so that you have about 35 minutes to review.

6) The most important instruction is to *read each question* and make sure you know what is wanted. The second most important instruction is to *time yourself properly* so that you answer every question. The third most important instruction is to *answer every question*. Guess if you have to but include something for each question. Remember that you will receive no credit for a blank and will probably receive some credit if you write something in answer to an essay question. If you guess a letter – say "B" for a multiple-choice question – you may have guessed right. If you leave a blank as an answer to a multiple-choice question, the examiners may respect your feelings but it will not add a point to your score. Some exams may penalize you for wrong answers, so in such cases *only*, you may not want to guess unless you have some basis for your answer.

7) Suggestions
    a. Objective-type questions
        1. Examine the question booklet for proper sequence of pages and questions
        2. Read all instructions carefully
        3. Skip any question which seems too difficult; return to it after all other questions have been answered
        4. Apportion your time properly; do not spend too much time on any single question or group of questions

5. Note and underline key words – *all, most, fewest, least, best, worst, same, opposite,* etc.
6. Pay particular attention to negatives
7. Note unusual option, e.g., unduly long, short, complex, different or similar in content to the body of the question
8. Observe the use of "hedging" words – *probably, may, most likely,* etc.
9. Make sure that your answer is put next to the same number as the question
10. Do not second-guess unless you have good reason to believe the second answer is definitely more correct
11. Cross out original answer if you decide another answer is more accurate; do not erase until you are ready to hand your paper in
12. Answer all questions; guess unless instructed otherwise
13. Leave time for review

   b. Essay questions
1. Read each question carefully
2. Determine exactly what is wanted. Underline key words or phrases.
3. Decide on outline or paragraph answer
4. Include many different points and elements unless asked to develop any one or two points or elements
5. Show impartiality by giving pros and cons unless directed to select one side only
6. Make and write down any assumptions you find necessary to answer the questions
7. Watch your English, grammar, punctuation and choice of words
8. Time your answers; don't crowd material

8) Answering the essay question

Most essay questions can be answered by framing the specific response around several key words or ideas. Here are a few such key words or ideas:

M's: manpower, materials, methods, money, management
P's: purpose, program, policy, plan, procedure, practice, problems, pitfalls, personnel, public relations

   a. Six basic steps in handling problems:
1. Preliminary plan and background development
2. Collect information, data and facts
3. Analyze and interpret information, data and facts
4. Analyze and develop solutions as well as make recommendations
5. Prepare report and sell recommendations
6. Install recommendations and follow up effectiveness

   b. Pitfalls to avoid
1. *Taking things for granted* – A statement of the situation does not necessarily imply that each of the elements is necessarily true; for example, a complaint may be invalid and biased so that all that can be taken for granted is that a complaint has been registered

2. *Considering only one side of a situation* – Wherever possible, indicate several alternatives and then point out the reasons you selected the best one
3. *Failing to indicate follow up* – Whenever your answer indicates action on your part, make certain that you will take proper follow-up action to see how successful your recommendations, procedures or actions turn out to be
4. *Taking too long in answering any single question* – Remember to time your answers properly

IX. AFTER THE TEST

Scoring procedures differ in detail among civil service jurisdictions although the general principles are the same. Whether the papers are hand-scored or graded by machine we have described, they are nearly always graded by number. That is, the person who marks the paper knows only the number – never the name – of the applicant. Not until all the papers have been graded will they be matched with names. If other tests, such as training and experience or oral interview ratings have been given, scores will be combined. Different parts of the examination usually have different weights. For example, the written test might count 60 percent of the final grade, and a rating of training and experience 40 percent. In many jurisdictions, veterans will have a certain number of points added to their grades.

After the final grade has been determined, the names are placed in grade order and an eligible list is established. There are various methods for resolving ties between those who get the same final grade – probably the most common is to place first the name of the person whose application was received first. Job offers are made from the eligible list in the order the names appear on it. You will be notified of your grade and your rank as soon as all these computations have been made. This will be done as rapidly as possible.

People who are found to meet the requirements in the announcement are called "eligibles." Their names are put on a list of eligible candidates. An eligible's chances of getting a job depend on how high he stands on this list and how fast agencies are filling jobs from the list.

When a job is to be filled from a list of eligibles, the agency asks for the names of people on the list of eligibles for that job. When the civil service commission receives this request, it sends to the agency the names of the three people highest on this list. Or, if the job to be filled has specialized requirements, the office sends the agency the names of the top three persons who meet these requirements from the general list.

The appointing officer makes a choice from among the three people whose names were sent to him. If the selected person accepts the appointment, the names of the others are put back on the list to be considered for future openings.

That is the rule in hiring from all kinds of eligible lists, whether they are for typist, carpenter, chemist, or something else. For every vacancy, the appointing officer has his choice of any one of the top three eligibles on the list. This explains why the person whose name is on top of the list sometimes does not get an appointment when some of the persons lower on the list do. If the appointing officer chooses the second or third eligible, the No. 1 eligible does not get a job at once, but stays on the list until he is appointed or the list is terminated.

X. HOW TO PASS THE INTERVIEW TEST

The examination for which you applied requires an oral interview test. You have already taken the written test and you are now being called for the interview test – the final part of the formal examination.

You may think that it is not possible to prepare for an interview test and that there are no procedures to follow during an interview. Our purpose is to point out some things you can do in advance that will help you and some good rules to follow and pitfalls to avoid while you are being interviewed.

What is an interview supposed to test?

The written examination is designed to test the technical knowledge and competence of the candidate; the oral is designed to evaluate intangible qualities, not readily measured otherwise, and to establish a list showing the relative fitness of each candidate – as measured against his competitors – for the position sought. Scoring is not on the basis of "right" and "wrong," but on a sliding scale of values ranging from "not passable" to "outstanding." As a matter of fact, it is possible to achieve a relatively low score without a single "incorrect" answer because of evident weakness in the qualities being measured.

Occasionally, an examination may consist entirely of an oral test – either an individual or a group oral. In such cases, information is sought concerning the technical knowledges and abilities of the candidate, since there has been no written examination for this purpose. More commonly, however, an oral test is used to supplement a written examination.

Who conducts interviews?

The composition of oral boards varies among different jurisdictions. In nearly all, a representative of the personnel department serves as chairman. One of the members of the board may be a representative of the department in which the candidate would work. In some cases, "outside experts" are used, and, frequently, a businessman or some other representative of the general public is asked to serve. Labor and management or other special groups may be represented. The aim is to secure the services of experts in the appropriate field.

However the board is composed, it is a good idea (and not at all improper or unethical) to ascertain in advance of the interview who the members are and what groups they represent. When you are introduced to them, you will have some idea of their backgrounds and interests, and at least you will not stutter and stammer over their names.

What should be done before the interview?

While knowledge about the board members is useful and takes some of the surprise element out of the interview, there is other preparation which is more substantive. It *is* possible to prepare for an oral interview – in several ways:

1) Keep a copy of your application and review it carefully before the interview

This may be the only document before the oral board, and the starting point of the interview. Know what education and experience you have listed there, and the sequence and dates of all of it. Sometimes the board will ask you to review the highlights of your experience for them; you should not have to hem and haw doing it.

2) Study the class specification and the examination announcement

Usually, the oral board has one or both of these to guide them. The qualities, characteristics or knowledges required by the position sought are stated in these documents. They offer valuable clues as to the nature of the oral interview. For example, if the job involves supervisory responsibilities, the announcement will usually indicate that knowledge of modern supervisory methods and the qualifications of the candidate as a supervisor will be tested. If so, you can expect such questions, frequently in the form of a hypothetical situation which you are expected to solve. NEVER go into an oral without knowledge of the duties and responsibilities of the job you seek.

3) Think through each qualification required

Try to visualize the kind of questions you would ask if you were a board member. How well could you answer them? Try especially to appraise your own knowledge and background in each area, *measured against the job sought*, and identify any areas in which you are weak. Be critical and realistic – do not flatter yourself.

4) Do some general reading in areas in which you feel you may be weak

For example, if the job involves supervision and your past experience has NOT, some general reading in supervisory methods and practices, particularly in the field of human relations, might be useful. Do NOT study agency procedures or detailed manuals. The oral board will be testing your understanding and capacity, not your memory.

5) Get a good night's sleep and watch your general health and mental attitude

You will want a clear head at the interview. Take care of a cold or any other minor ailment, and of course, no hangovers.

What should be done on the day of the interview?

Now comes the day of the interview itself. Give yourself plenty of time to get there. Plan to arrive somewhat ahead of the scheduled time, particularly if your appointment is in the fore part of the day. If a previous candidate fails to appear, the board might be ready for you a bit early. By early afternoon an oral board is almost invariably behind schedule if there are many candidates, and you may have to wait. Take along a book or magazine to read, or your application to review, but leave any extraneous material in the waiting room when you go in for your interview. In any event, relax and compose yourself.

The matter of dress is important. The board is forming impressions about you – from your experience, your manners, your attitude, and your appearance. Give your personal appearance careful attention. Dress your best, but not your flashiest. Choose conservative, appropriate clothing, and be sure it is immaculate. This is a business interview, and your appearance should indicate that you regard it as such. Besides, being well groomed and properly dressed will help boost your confidence.

Sooner or later, someone will call your name and escort you into the interview room. *This is it.* From here on you are on your own. It is too late for any more preparation. But remember, you asked for this opportunity to prove your fitness, and you are here because your request was granted.

What happens when you go in?

The usual sequence of events will be as follows: The clerk (who is often the board stenographer) will introduce you to the chairman of the oral board, who will introduce you to the other members of the board. Acknowledge the introductions before you sit down. Do not be surprised if you find a microphone facing you or a stenotypist sitting by. Oral interviews are usually recorded in the event of an appeal or other review.

Usually the chairman of the board will open the interview by reviewing the highlights of your education and work experience from your application – primarily for the benefit of the other members of the board, as well as to get the material into the record. Do not interrupt or comment unless there is an error or significant misinterpretation; if that is the case, do not hesitate. But do not quibble about insignificant matters. Also, he will usually ask you some question about your education, experience or your present job – partly to get you to start talking and to establish the interviewing "rapport." He may start the actual questioning, or turn it over to one of the other members. Frequently, each member undertakes the questioning on a particular area, one in which he is perhaps most competent, so you can expect each member to participate in the examination. Because time is limited, you may also expect some rather abrupt switches in the direction the questioning takes, so do not be upset by it. Normally, a board member will not pursue a single line of questioning unless he discovers a particular strength or weakness.

After each member has participated, the chairman will usually ask whether any member has any further questions, then will ask you if you have anything you wish to add. Unless you are expecting this question, it may floor you. Worse, it may start you off on an extended, extemporaneous speech. The board is not usually seeking more information. The question is principally to offer you a last opportunity to present further qualifications or to indicate that you have nothing to add. So, if you feel that a significant qualification or characteristic has been overlooked, it is proper to point it out in a sentence or so. Do not compliment the board on the thoroughness of their examination – they have been sketchy, and you know it. If you wish, merely say, "No thank you, I have nothing further to add." This is a point where you can "talk yourself out" of a good impression or fail to present an important bit of information. Remember, *you close the interview yourself.*

The chairman will then say, "That is all, Mr. _____, thank you." Do not be startled; the interview is over, and quicker than you think. Thank him, gather your belongings and take your leave. Save your sigh of relief for the other side of the door.

How to put your best foot forward

Throughout this entire process, you may feel that the board individually and collectively is trying to pierce your defenses, seek out your hidden weaknesses and embarrass and confuse you. Actually, this is not true. They are obliged to make an appraisal of your qualifications for the job you are seeking, and they want to see you in your best light. Remember, they must interview all candidates and a non-cooperative candidate may become a failure in spite of their best efforts to bring out his qualifications. Here are 15 suggestions that will help you:

1) Be natural – Keep your attitude confident, not cocky

If you are not confident that you can do the job, do not expect the board to be. Do not apologize for your weaknesses, try to bring out your strong points. The board is interested in a positive, not negative, presentation. Cockiness will antagonize any board member and make him wonder if you are covering up a weakness by a false show of strength.

2) Get comfortable, but don't lounge or sprawl

Sit erectly but not stiffly. A careless posture may lead the board to conclude that you are careless in other things, or at least that you are not impressed by the importance of the occasion. Either conclusion is natural, even if incorrect. Do not fuss with your clothing, a pencil or an ashtray. Your hands may occasionally be useful to emphasize a point; do not let them become a point of distraction.

3) Do not wisecrack or make small talk

This is a serious situation, and your attitude should show that you consider it as such. Further, the time of the board is limited – they do not want to waste it, and neither should you.

4) Do not exaggerate your experience or abilities

In the first place, from information in the application or other interviews and sources, the board may know more about you than you think. Secondly, you probably will not get away with it. An experienced board is rather adept at spotting such a situation, so do not take the chance.

5) If you know a board member, do not make a point of it, yet do not hide it

Certainly you are not fooling him, and probably not the other members of the board. Do not try to take advantage of your acquaintanceship – it will probably do you little good.

6) Do not dominate the interview

Let the board do that. They will give you the clues – do not assume that you have to do all the talking. Realize that the board has a number of questions to ask you, and do not try to take up all the interview time by showing off your extensive knowledge of the answer to the first one.

7) Be attentive

You only have 20 minutes or so, and you should keep your attention at its sharpest throughout. When a member is addressing a problem or question to you, give him your undivided attention. Address your reply principally to him, but do not exclude the other board members.

8) Do not interrupt

A board member may be stating a problem for you to analyze. He will ask you a question when the time comes. Let him state the problem, and wait for the question.

9) Make sure you understand the question

Do not try to answer until you are sure what the question is. If it is not clear, restate it in your own words or ask the board member to clarify it for you. However, do not haggle about minor elements.

10) Reply promptly but not hastily

A common entry on oral board rating sheets is "candidate responded readily," or "candidate hesitated in replies." Respond as promptly and quickly as you can, but do not jump to a hasty, ill-considered answer.

11) Do not be peremptory in your answers

A brief answer is proper – but do not fire your answer back. That is a losing game from your point of view. The board member can probably ask questions much faster than you can answer them.

12) Do not try to create the answer you think the board member wants

He is interested in what kind of mind you have and how it works – not in playing games. Furthermore, he can usually spot this practice and will actually grade you down on it.

13) Do not switch sides in your reply merely to agree with a board member

Frequently, a member will take a contrary position merely to draw you out and to see if you are willing and able to defend your point of view. Do not start a debate, yet do not surrender a good position. If a position is worth taking, it is worth defending.

14) Do not be afraid to admit an error in judgment if you are shown to be wrong

The board knows that you are forced to reply without any opportunity for careful consideration. Your answer may be demonstrably wrong. If so, admit it and get on with the interview.

15) Do not dwell at length on your present job

The opening question may relate to your present assignment. Answer the question but do not go into an extended discussion. You are being examined for a *new* job, not your present one. As a matter of fact, try to phrase ALL your answers in terms of the job for which you are being examined.

Basis of Rating

Probably you will forget most of these "do's" and "don'ts" when you walk into the oral interview room. Even remembering them all will not ensure you a passing grade. Perhaps you did not have the qualifications in the first place. But remembering them will help you to put your best foot forward, without treading on the toes of the board members.

Rumor and popular opinion to the contrary notwithstanding, an oral board wants you to make the best appearance possible. They know you are under pressure – but they also want to see how you respond to it as a guide to what your reaction would be under the pressures of the job you seek. They will be influenced by the degree of poise you display, the personal traits you show and the manner in which you respond.

ABOUT THIS BOOK

This book contains tests divided into Examination Sections. Go through each test, answering every question in the margin. We have also attached a sample answer sheet at the back of the book that can be removed and used. At the end of each test look at the answer key and check your answers. On the ones you got wrong, look at the right answer choice and learn. Do not fill in the answers first. Do not memorize the questions and answers, but understand the answer and principles involved. On your test, the questions will likely be different from the samples. Questions are changed and new ones added. If you understand these past questions you should have success with any changes that arise. Tests may consist of several types of questions. We have additional books on each subject should more study be advisable or necessary for you. Finally, the more you study, the better prepared you will be. This book is intended to be the last thing you study before you walk into the examination room. Prior study of relevant texts is also recommended. NLC publishes some of these in our Fundamental Series. Knowledge and good sense are important factors in passing your exam. Good luck also helps. So now study this Passbook, absorb the material contained within and take that knowledge into the examination. Then do your best to pass that exam.

EXAMINATION SECTION

EXAMINATION SECTION
TEST 1

DIRECTIONS: Each question or incomplete statement is followed by several suggested answers or completions. Select the one that BEST answers the question or completes the statement. *PRINT THE LETTER OF THE CORRECT ANSWER IN THE SPACE AT THE RIGHT.*

1. In medical terms, a word that ends with the suffix "-emia" is an object or condition related to the

    A. brain stem
    B. lymph
    C. endocrine system
    D. blood

2. Chondralgia is a term that describes pain in or around the

    A. bone
    B. tendons
    C. cartilage
    D. teeth

3. The medical term used to describe difficult or labored breathing is

    A. pneumospasm
    B. dyspnea
    C. pleurisy
    D. apnea

4. The sclera is the

    A. curved, transparent layer that covers the front part of the eye and protects its inner structures
    B. collection of blood vessels in the rear of the eye that oxygenate the retina
    C. white outer covering of the eye
    D. membrane that covers the eye and lines the inside of the eyelids, and helps lubricate the eye by producing mucus and tears

ICD-9-CM

5. A pregnant woman is found to have a streptococcal infection of the urinary tract. What is the correct diagnosis code?

    A. 599.1,041.1
    B. 599.0,041.0,646.60
    C. 646.60,599.0,041.0
    D. 599.8,041.0

6. Code for acute left-sided CVA with infarct resulting in hemiplegia, right side. The patient is right-handed.

    A. 434.9,3432.1
    B. 342.90,434.91
    C. 434.91,342.90
    D. 434.91,342.91

7. A patient has hypertensive retinopathy. The diagnosis states that the patient's hypertension is malignant. The correct diagnostic code is

   A. 401.0
   B. 401.0, 352.10
   C. 362.11, 401.0
   D. 362.11

8. In a diagnostic statement following a recent accident, the report does not state where the accident occurred. The coder should

   A. not use a Place of Occurrence E-code
   B. avoid the use of any E-codes for this diagnosis
   C. use E849.0
   D. use E849.9

9. Each of the following V codes is acceptable ONLY as a primary or principal diagnosis, EXCEPT

   A. V46
   B. V22.0
   C. V70
   D. V58.3

10. ICD-9-CM serves several major functions for insurance purposes. Which of the following is NOT one of them?

    A. To assist in establishing medical necessity for services and procedures
    B. To enable providers to report non-physician services such as durable medical equipment, ambulance services, supplies and medications.
    C. To justify procedures and services rendered by the physician
    D. To serve as an indicator in measuring the quality of health care delivered by the provider

Evaluation & Management

11. What range of codes are used to report Evaluation and Management (E/M) services furnished to a patient residing in his or her own private residence?

    A. 99211-99215
    B. 99321-99353
    C. 99341-99350
    D. 99455-99456

12. A physician evaluates a new patient for lower-right quadrant pain that is accompanied by nausea, vomiting, and a low-grade fever. The physician obtained surgical consultation and it was suggested that the patient be kept overnight to rule out the possibility of a ruptured appendix.
    Based on the information above, the LEAST appropriate E&M code for this visit is

    A. 99218
    B. 99219
    C. 99220
    D. 99221

13. Which of the following modifiers is NOT applicable to E & M? 13.____

    A. 21
    B. 25
    C. 27
    D. 52

14. "Past history" includes each of the following components, EXCEPT 14.____

    A. current medications
    B. prior hospitalizations
    C. occupational history
    D. allergies

Anesthesia

15. Which of the following is a general obstetrical anesthesia code? 15.____

    A. 01960
    B. 01967
    C. 01969
    D. 01991

16. Prior to the performance of anterior cruciate ligament (ACL) surgery, in which all but the patella tendon harvest is done arthroscopically, the anesthesiologist provides the necessary anesthesia to the knee joint. The anesthesia code for this procedure is 16.____

    A. 00128
    B. 01320
    C. 01382
    D. 01402

17. Code for anesthesia complicated by utilization of controlled hypotension. 17.____

    A. 62278
    B. 62279
    C. 99135
    D. 99140

Surgery & Modifiers

18. A rubber vaginal pessary is inserted to treat a prolapsed uterus. The procedural code is 18.____

    A. A4560
    B. A4561
    C. A4562
    D. A4563

19. Code for a flexible sigmoidoscopy, with biopsy, performed to screen for colorectal cancer. 19.____

    A. 45330, 45331
    B. 45340
    C. 45331, 45345
    D. 45331, G0104

20. Code for the paring of two calluses on the leg.

    A. 11055, 11055-59
    B. 11055 x 2
    C. 11056
    D. 11057

21. A patient undergoes an endoscopy of the small intestine, beyond the second portion of the duodenum, not including the ileum, twice in one day. The second procedure is performed by a different physician. The appropriate coding for these procedures would be

    A. 44366 x 2
    B. 44366, 44366-59
    C. 44366, 44366-76
    D. 44366, 44366-77

22. During one surgical session, the surgeon repairs a rotator cuff, a ligament release, and a claviculectomy. The most appropriate way to code for this service is

    A. 23412, 23415, 23120
    B. 23412, 23415-51, 23120-51
    C. 23412, 23415-59, 23120-59
    D. 23412, 23415, 23120-51

23. A surgeon performs a revision of a mastoidectomy that results in a modified radical mastoidectomy. The code for this procedure would be

    A. 69505
    B. 69602
    C. 69603
    D. 69511

24. Which of the following modifiers is NOT applicable to surgery?

    A. 22
    B. 25
    C. 50
    D. 77

25. Which of the following modifiers is "informational only" and is does not impact payment?

    A. 22
    B. 25
    C. 32
    D. 51

Radiology

26. Which of the following is a radiologic procedure that allows the viewing of a single plane of the body by blurring out all but the desired field?

    A. Ultrasound
    B. Tomography
    C. Densitometry
    D. Magnetic Resonance Imaging (MRI)

27. A patient who has been diagnosed with a pericardial clot is admitted to the hospital. The physician orders an ultrasound B-scan of the chest and an MRI without contrast medium, and then performs a pericardiotomy to remove the clot. The appropriate procedural codes would be

    A. 76604, 71550, 33020
    B. 76856, 71560, 33020
    C. 76645, 71550, 33025
    D. 76604, 71550, 33025

28. In a spine projection that focuses on the C-5 to T-6 vertebrae, a technician usually asks the patient to assume what is known at the _____ position.

    A. swimmer's
    B. Trendlenburg
    C. tangential
    D. apical-lordotic

29. Which of the following modifiers is NOT applicable to radiology?

    A. 22
    B. 50
    C. 78
    D. 99

Pathology & Laboratory

30. After a patient passes a kidney stone, a pathologist conducts both a gross and a microscopic examination on the calculus to determine the presence or absence of disease. The procedural code for this examination is

    A. 88300
    B. 88302
    C. 88305
    D. 88309

31. A newborn's blood glucose is tested by reagent strip after a heel stick is performed. The correct coding for this procedure is

    A. 82948, 36416
    B. 82962, 36415
    C. 82947
    D. 82948

32. Code for a full lipid panel.

    A. 82465, 83718, 84478
    B. 82947, 80061
    C. 80061
    D. 85025, 80061

Medicine

33. Code for a rhythm ECG with two leads, with interpretation and report.

    A. 93000
    B. 93040
    C. 93040, 93042
    D. 93230

34. In a family physician's office, a patient has two common warts and two plantar warts cryosurgically removed. The appropriate coding for these procedures would be:

    A. 17000, 17003
    B. 17110
    C. 17110, 17111
    D. 17000, 17003, 17003, 17003

35. The best way to define the difference between modifier and the prolonged services codes (99354-99355) is to say that modifier 21 may

    A. only be attached to the highest level code in a given family of E/M services, while the prolonged services codes may be used with any level of service
    B. be used when time is considered the controlling factor in your E/M code selection, while the prolonged services codes may not
    C. may only be used with E/M codes for office visits, while the prolonged services codes may only be used with codes for hospital visits
    D. may be used interchangeably with prolonged services codes

36. Aphakia is

    A. a cleansing of the blood outside of the body
    B. a rapid, involuntary movement of the eye
    C. the absence of the lens of the eye
    D. the movement of the eye that corresponds to the movement of objects in the visual field

37. Which of the following is a device for detecting color-blindness?

    A. Anomaloscope
    B. Keratograph
    C. Ophthalmoscope
    D. Adaptometer

38. During a partial hospitalization visit, a patient attends an individual psychiatry session to modify her obsessive behavior and discuss some events from her childhood. During the session, which lasts 80 minutes, the psychiatrist checks the patient's blood lithium levels and evaluates her diabetes. The most appropriate code for this visit would be

    A. 90809
    B. 90815
    C. 90822
    D. 90829

HCPCS

39. What is the code for a surgical tray?

    A. 99075
    B. A4550
    C. A4670
    D. E0950

40. A patient received occupational therapy for a total of 60 minutes. The correct coding for this is

    A. 97530 x 2
    B. 97530 x 4
    C. 97740 x 4
    D. 97012

41. HCPCS B codes may denote

    A. surgical dressings
    B. parenteral and enteral nutrition
    C. optical supplies/lenses
    D. inhalation drugs

42. The main difference between HCPCS Level II codes and CPT codes is that HCPCS Level II codes

    A. do not allow for the addition of modifiers
    B. may have from 3 to 6 digits
    C. end with a letter
    D. begin with a letter

Medical Tests & Devices

43. Patients who have an aneurysm, but for whom surgery presents too high a risk, often have a(n) _____ implanted within the aneurysm in order to relieve pressure on the weakened artery wall.

    A. guide wire
    B. shunt
    C. catheter
    D. stent graft

44. Spirometry is a pulmonary function test. One of the things it is designed to measure is

    A. gas dilution, or the rate at which oxygen and other gases are absorbed by the alveoli
    B. total lung capacity, or the maximum amount of air your lungs can hold when fully inflated.
    C. residual volume, or the amount of air that remains in the lungs after a person has exhaled as completely as possible
    D. forced expiratory volume, or the amount of air a person can exhale forcefully in a sustained breath

Anatomy

45. The coronary arteries

    A. dilate and contract in rhythm with the heart ventricles
    B. branch from the pulmonary veins
    C. are the first branch from the base of the aorta
    D. supply part of the heart muscle with oxygen

46. Which of the following is NOT one of the three auditory bones?

    A. Incus
    B. Stapes
    C. Utricle
    D. Malleus

CPT & HCPCS Level II Conventions

47. When an open biopsy is followed by a more extensive and definitive procedure, the coder should report

    A. the more extensive procedure and the open procedure
    B. the open biopsy
    C. only the extensive procedure
    D. only the procedure that produces a diagnosis

48. If a procedure is complicated by the late effects of a previous surgery, irradiation, infection or very low birth weight, and there is no separate CPT code to identify these, the coder should use modifier

    A. 21
    B. 22
    C. 55
    D. 79

49. Category III CPT codes

    A. refer to emerging technology
    B. are the existing set of codes that were developed in 1966
    C. are used as a measure of performance
    D. correlate with DRGs

50. During an evaluation and management visit, a surgeon makes the decision to perform surgery. The CPT code for this encounter should include modifier

    A. 24
    B. 52
    C. 57
    D. 79

KEY (CORRECT ANSWERS)

1. D	11. C	21. D	31. A	41. B
2. C	12. D	22. B	32. C	42. D
3. B	13. D	23. B	33. B	43. D
4. C	14. C	24. B	34. D	44. D
5. C	15. A	25. C	35. A	45. C
6. D	16. C	26. B	36. C	46. C
7. C	17. C	27. A	37. A	47. A
8. A	18. B	28. A	38. C	48. B
9. A	19. D	29. C	39. B	49. A
10. B	20. C	30. B	40. B	50. C

TEST 2

DIRECTIONS: Each question or incomplete statement is followed by several suggested answers or completions. Select the one that BEST answers the question or completes the statement. *PRINT THE LETTER OF THE CORRECT ANSWER IN THE SPACE AT THE RIGHT.*

Medical Terminology

1. The medical term that denotes an abnormally slow heartbeat is

   A. tachycardia
   B. bradycardia
   C. myocardia
   D. atrial fibrillation

2. In medical terms, "-megaly" is a suffix meaning

   A. toward the midline
   B. soft or softening
   C. enlarged
   D. one-thousandth

3. The epididymis is a

   A. muscular tube that moves sperm from the testicle to the ejaculatory duct
   B. gland on the posterior surface of the urinary bladder that secretes a significant proportion of the fluid that ultimately becomes semen
   C. sac of skin and muscle containing the testicles
   D. narrow, tightly-coiled tube connecting the efferent ducts from the rear of each testicle to its vas deferens

ICD-9-CM

4. A patient visits a physician and undergoes a series of tests, after which the physician diagnoses him with arteriosclerotic cardiovascular disease. The correct diagnosis code for this encounter is

   A. 402.9, 440.0
   B. 440.9, 429.2
   C. 429.2, 440.8
   D. 429.2, 440.9

5. Code for meningitis attributable to Lyme disease.

   A. 320.9, 087.1
   B. 320.9, 088.81
   C. 320.8, 088.81
   D. 320.7, 088.81

6. A written diagnosis includes primary systemic hypertension, malignant, as well as congestive heart failure and renal failure. The physician has not explicitly stated that there is a link between the hypertension and the heart or renal disease. The best diagnostic code for this patient is

   A. 401.0, 402.01, 404.00
   B. 404.03
   C. 401.0, 404.3
   D. 404.03, 429.1, 585

7. ICD-9-CM codes labeled "NEC" or "NOS" should be used

   A. only when neither the diagnostic statement nor a thorough review of the medical record provides adequate information to permit assignment of a more specific code
   B. when either "NEC" or "NOS" is specifically used by the physician in the diagnostic statement
   C. when a condition is specified, but no separate code for that condition is provided
   D. when a code does for a specific condition cannot be found in the Tabular List

8. The term "Parkinson's disease" is an example of a(n)

   A. late effect
   B. anagram
   C. eponym
   D. subcategory

9. In ICD-9-CM, slanted square brackets [ ] are used

   A. in the tabular list to reduce repetitive wording by connecting a series of terms on the left with a statement on the right
   B. only in the alphabetic index, to enclose a second code number that must be used with the first, and is always sequenced second.
   C. only in the tabular list to enclose synonyms, alternative wordings, and explanatory phrases.
   D. to indicate a footnote that normally means a fifth digit is needed in that category

Evaluation & Management

10. A physician examines a 43-year-old new male patient for a contusion of the knee. The history and examination are problem focused. There are minimal diagnosis and management options, minimal data, and the doctor's decision involves straightforward decision-making.
    Based on the information above, the most appropriate E&M code for this visit is

    A. 99201
    B. 99202
    C. 99212
    D. 99213

11. A physician sees a new patient in her office. She performs and documents an expanded problem-focused history, expanded problem-focused exam, and has moderate complexity medical decision making. The nature of the presenting problem is moderate complexity, and the physician spends thirty-five minutes face-to-face with the patient. Of the total time spent, the physician spent 20 minutes counseling the patient on the disease process, discussing treatment options and coordinating consultations with other physicians. The most appropriate E&M code for this visit is

    A. 99200
    B. 99201
    C. 99203
    D. 99214

12. A 4-year-old girl has been hospitalized with viral pneumonia for several days. On Thursday, the girl developed a fever of 102°F. In a subsequent hospital visit, the attending physician performed a problem-focused history and examination. The medical decision making was low-complexity. The most appropriate E&M code for this subsequent visit by the attending physician is

    A. 99220
    B. 99222
    C. 99231
    D. 99262

13. "Review of Systems" includes each of the following components, EXCEPT

    A. eyes
    B. psychiatric
    C. chiropractic
    D. hemic/lymphatic

14. The subjective information the patient gives the physician during an E & M visit is the

    A. examination
    B. history
    C. nature of the presenting problem
    D. SOAP

Anesthesia

15. Anesthesia codes are grouped by

    A. procedure
    B. substance
    C. anatomical site
    D. route of introduction

16. Prior to performing an otoscopy on a patient's inner ear, a physician administers the necessary anesthesia. The appropriate anesthesia code is

    A. 00120
    B. 00124
    C. 00126
    D. 0014

Surgery & Modifiers

17. In the same session, a surgeon performs cataract surgery (standard extracapsular cataract removal with insertion of intraocular lens prosthesis) and trabeculectomy. In a Medicare claim, the correct CPT coding is

    A. 66984
    B. 66984, 66170
    C. 66170, 66984-51, V2630
    D. 66170, 66984-51

18. A physician repaired a broken leg and a broken arm in the same operative session. The correct procedural code for this service is

    A. 27766-77
    B. 27766, 25620-59-51
    C. 27766, 25620-59, 25620-51
    D. 27766, 2620-54

19. While finishing surgery on the acromioclavicular (AC) joint, the surgeon inserts an implantable infusion pain pump, which is specified as a pump and not simply a catheter. The procedure code for this placement would be

    A. 11981
    B. 23929
    C. 37202
    D. the procedure is considered part of the surgery and would not be coded

20. A surgeon performs open treatment of a femoral fracture by placing a pin in the proximal end neck. Later, while in the recovery room, the pin is dislodged, and the surgeon must repeat the procedure. This should be coded

    A. 27236 x 2
    B. 27236, 27236-59
    C. 27236, 27236-76
    D. 27236, 27236-77

21. Code for the direct ligation of esophageal varices.

    A. 43331
    B. 43400
    C. 43341
    D. 43350

22. The preoperative period included in the global fee for major surgery is

    A. 0 day
    B. 1 day
    C. 0 to 10 days, depending on the procedure
    D. 3 days

23. Code for a laparoscopic cholecystectomy with exploration of the common duct.

    A. 47562, 47564-51
    B. 47564
    C. 47610
    D. 47620

24. Modifier 80 is used to report

    A. a service that has been partially reduced or eliminated at the physician's discretion
    B. the performance of an unrelated procedure or service during the postoperative period of another procedure or service
    C. the use of an outside laboratory
    D. surgical assistance services

Radiology

25. Retrograde cystography is a detailed radiologic examination of the

   A. lymph nodes
   B. spleen
   C. urinary bladder
   D. tumor

26. For billing purposes, the "technical component" of radiology does NOT include

   A. facility overhead in providing the service
   B. the physician's interpretation
   C. film and film processing
   D. the work of the technician

27. A physician submits documentation for billing a 45-year-old patient who has had an x-ray of both his left and right forearms. The correct coding for this procedure is

   A. 73090
   B. 73090, 73090-59
   C. 73090-50
   D. 73090-RT, 73090-LT

28. In the hospital, a radiologist performs an injection procedure and the supervision and interpretation specific to a cystography. The correct procedural coding would be

   A. 51600, 74430
   B. 51600, 74430-26
   C. 74450
   D. 51600, 74450

Pathology & Laboratory

29. Three separate wound cultures are initiated from three different anatomical sites on the same day. The correct way to code for this service is

   A. 87070, 87070-59, 87070-59
   B. 87070-91
   C. 87070-51
   D. 87070

30. Code for an automated urinalysis with microscopy.

   A. 81000
   B. 81001
   C. 81015
   D. 81020

31. Which of the following is NOT a common method for qualitative drug testing?

    A. High performance liquid chromatography (HPLC)
    B. "Peak and trough" assay
    C. Thin layer chromatography (TLC)
    D. Gas chromatography/mass spectrometry (GC/MS)

32. An 18-year-old swimmer presents to the emergency room with dizziness and fatigue. After the history and exam, the ER physician orders carbon dioxide, chloride potassium, sodium, and glucose tests to check for dehydration and hypoglycemia. The lab technician performs a blood draw and the glucose test is done using a reagent strip. The most appropriate coding for this visit is

    A. 80051, 36416
    B. 80051, 82948, 35415
    C. 80048, 82948, 36415
    D. 82374, 82435, 84132, 84295, 82948, 35415

Medicine

33. The range of codes that deals with gastroenterology is

    A. 91000-91299
    B. 92950-93278
    C. 94010-94799
    D. 90700-90749

34. A Medicare patient visits a physician's office for a B-12 injection. The patient is shown to an examination room and given the injection by a nurse with very little consultation. The most appropriate code for this visit is

    A. J3420, 99211-25
    B. J3420, 99211
    C. G0351, J3420
    D. 90782, J3420

35. When using trigger-point injection codes 20552 and 20553 appropriately, the coder will submit

    A. 20552 for the first two injections and 20553 for any additional injections
    B. 20552 for the first two muscles injected and then 20553 for additional muscles injected
    C. 20553 for each injection, if you at least three injections are performed
    D. 20552 one or two muscles are injected, or 20553 if three or more muscles are injected

36. A flu shot is given to a Medicare patient and is accompanied by a significant, separately identifiable evaluation and management service. Both services are provided by a nurse. The most appropriate coding for this encounter would be

    A. G0008 and 90658
    B. 90471, 90658, 99211-25
    C. G0008, 90658, 99211-25
    D. 90471, 90658]

37. The fatty tissue below the dermis is the

    A. subcutaneous
    B. epidermis
    C. epithelium
    D. carapace

HCPCS

38. If there is both a HCPCS Level II national code and a CPT code describing basically the same thing, the coder should use

    A. both codes, listing the CPT code first
    B. the HCPCS code for supplies and the CPT code for physician procedures
    C. the CPT code in all cases
    D. the HCPCS code in all cases

39. A patient was given a chemotherapy IV infusion using a single drug for seven hours. The correct code for this is

    A. G0347x 1 unit, G0360 x 6 units
    B. G0359 x 7 units
    C. G0359 x 1 unit, G0360 x 6 units
    D. 96422 x 1 unit, 99423 x 6 units

40. "Temporary assignment" codes in HCPCS may begin with each of the following, EXCEPT

    A. C   B. K   C. J   D. Q

41. HCPCS Level II codes include each of the following services that are not included in CPT, EXCEPT

    A. specific supplies
    B. durable medical equipment
    C. ambulance services
    D. neurological testing

Medical Tests & Devices

42. Which of the following tests is NOT typically used to screen for heart disease?

    A. Homocysteine
    B. Lipid panel
    C. Hematocrit
    D. Prothrombin time

43. A patient has a 12-lead ECG performed at 9:00 am. An ECG is ordered and repeated at noon, and again at 10:00 pm. This should be coded as

    A. 93000, 93000-76
    B. 93000, 93000, 93000
    C. 93000, 93000-76 x2
    D. 93000-76 x3

Anatomy

44. Each of the following muscles attaches to the collarbone, EXCEPT the

   A. pectoralis major
   B. subclavius
   C. trapezius
   D. supraspinus

45. The layer of the skin that lies just above the fascia of the underlying muscle is the

   A. sebaceous
   B. dermis
   C. subcutaneous
   D. papillary layer

CPT & HCPCS Level II Conventions

46. A patient is receiving general anesthesia. Modifier 23 should be used when the CPT manual, under the correct procedural code, notes that the procedure

   A. performed under "alternative anesthesia methods"
   B. is "usually performed without anesthesia or under local anesthesia"
   C. is performed "without anesthesia"
   D. is "usually performed under general anesthesia"

47. Which of the following is NOT a major section of CPT?

   A. Surgery
   B. Anesthesiology
   C. Modifiers
   D. Laboratory

48. The bullet (•) symbol is used in CPT to indicate

   A. a new code
   B. the descriptor for a code has changed since the prior revision of the CPT manual
   C. a minor surgical procedure not subject to a global fee
   D. a clinical example of an E & M code

49. The index at the back of the CPT manual allows the user to look up a code by each of the following means, EXCEPT by

   A. anatomical site
   B. symptom, common abbreviation, or eponym
   C. condition
   D. reimbursement rate

50. In the CPT manual, codes that have been deleted appear

   A. within a pair of facing triangles
   B. after a bullet•
   C. within parentheses ()
   D. within braces {}

KEY (CORRECT ANSWERS)

1. B	11. C	21. B	31. B	41. D
2. C	12. C	22. B	32. B	42. C
3. D	13. C	23. B	33. A	43. C
4. D	14. B	24. D	34. C	44. D
5. D	15. C	25. C	35. D	45. C
6. B	16. B	26. B	36. B	46. B
7. A	17. D	27. C	37. A	47. C
8. C	18. B	28. B	38. B	48. A
9. B	19. D	29. A	39. C	49. D
10. A	20. C	30. B	40. C	50. C

TEST 3

DIRECTIONS: Each question or incomplete statement is followed by several suggested answers or completions. Select the one that BEST answers the question or completes the statement. *PRINT THE LETTER OF THE CORRECT ANSWER IN THE SPACE AT THE RIGHT.*

Medical Terminology

1. The plural form of the word "sarcoma" is

   A. sarcomata
   B. sarcomae
   C. sarcomi
   D. sarcomaces

2. The medical term that describes an abnormal softening of brain tissue is

   A. encephalocele
   B. encephaloma
   C. encephalomalacia
   D. hydrocephalus

3. The medical abbreviation LMP stands for

   A. latent menopausal praxis
   B. last menstrual period
   C. lapsed medical policy
   D. lateromedial pulse

4. Episplenitis is a term denoting inflammation of the tissue _____ the spleen

   A. under
   B. over
   C. within
   D. behind

ICD-9-CM

5. A primary, malignant tumor of the throat would be coded

   A. 141.9
   B. 149.0
   C. 193
   D. 198.89

6. A teenage athlete, while playing soccer, suffered an acute tear of the anterior cruciate ligament in his right knee after a twisting injury. What is the correct diagnosis code?

   A. 717.83, 905.7, E929.8
   B. 844.1, E929.3
   C. 844.2, E888
   D. 844.2, E927

7. The V08 code should NOT be used if the term _____ is used in the diagnostic documentation.

   A. HIV-positive
   B. known HIV
   C. AIDS
   D. asymptomatic

8. A patient was admitted to a skilled nursing facility for intensive physical therapy rehabilitation for severe ataxia and blurry vision due to a recent stroke. The most appropriate diagnostic coding would be

   A. 438.7, 438.84
   B. V57.9, 438.7, 438.84
   C. V57.9, 438.7, 368.8, 438.84
   D. V57.1, 438.7, 368.8, 438.84

9. In the physician's notes, the patient's diastolic blood pressure is consistently higher than 120, and the patient is also experiencing renal failure. The best course of action would be for the coder to

   A. consult the physician about whether the patient's hypertension is malignant
   B. code the hypertension as terminal
   C. consult the physician about whether the patient's hypertension is unspecified
   D. code the hypertension as unspecified

10. Fifth digits are required on all diabetes mellitus codes. For Type II diabetes that is uncontrolled, the fifth digit would be

    A. 0   B. 1   C. 2   D. 3

Evaluation & Management

11. A patient comes in for a scheduled annual exam, but during the exam, the physician finds a skin rash that requires special medication. Based on this information, the most appropriate E&M code for this visit is

    A. 99397, 99214-25
    B. 99397, 99214
    C. 99397
    D. 99214

12. An 11-year-old girl who is an established patient comes into the office complaining of itching in her left leg. The itching is constant, and has been bothering her for two days, ever since she took a walk in the woods behind her home. The skin of her leg has patchy red areas with vesicular eruptions. The right leg appears normal. Her vital signs are normal, and her gait is unaffected. The physician diagnoses her with poison ivy and prescribes a topical corticosteroid cream. The correct diagnosis and procedural code for this encounter is

    A. 691.8, 99212   B. 691.8, 99213
    C. 692.6, 99212   D. 692.6, 99213

13. Medical decision making includes all of the following, EXCEPT   13.____

    A. treatment
    B. past medical history
    C. risk
    D. diagnosis

14. "Nature of the presenting problem" includes each of the following components, EXCEPT   14.____

    A. complaint
    B. allergies
    C. symptom
    D. sign

Anesthesia

15. A P3 modifier to an anesthesia code denotes a patient   15.____

    A. with mild systemic disease
    B. with severe systemic disease
    C. with systemic disease that is a constant threat to life
    D. who is not expected to survive without the given procedure

16. The type of anesthesia used to manage postoperative pain is   16.____

    A. regional block
    B. general anesthesia
    C. conscious sedation
    D. patient-controlled analgesia

17. An epidural anesthesia is administered for six hours during a cesarean delivery. The   17.____
    claim should be submitted using the following code:

    A. 99140
    B. S4850
    C. 01967
    D. 01967-23, 01968

Surgery & Modifiers

18. A patient is admitted to the emergency room with the following superficial knife wounds: 18.____
    2.1 cm on the scalp, 27.8 cm on the upper chest, 8.8 cm on the arm. The physician per-
    forms a simple closure of each of these wounds. The appropriate code for all of these
    procedures is

    A. 12001
    B. 12007
    C. 12001, 12004, 12007
    D. 12007, 12004, 12001

19. A physician performs an arthroscopic procedure to relieve median nerve compression at the wrist. After this procedure is found to have failed, the physician later performs an open procedure. The code for this procedure would be

    A. 29848
    B. 29848, 64721
    C. 64721-22
    D. 64721

20. A Medicare patient had a benign lesion measuring 1.5 cm removed from his back at his physician's office. The correct procedural code for this service is

    A. 11400
    B. 11400-57
    C. 11600-57
    D. 11700

21. A physician aspirates cysts on the right and left breasts during the same operative session. The procedure would be coded

    A. 19000-RT, 19000-LT
    B. 19000-50
    C. 19000, 19000-51
    D. 19102

22. When pyeloplasty is performed,

    A. an incision is made in the ureter
    B. an opening into the renal pelvis is surgically created
    C. a stent is inserted into the bladder and ureter(s)
    D. the renal pelvis is surgically reconstructed

23. Which of the following services is NOT included in the payment amount for a global surgical procedure?

    A. Postsurgical pain management
    B. The initial consultation or evaluation of the problem by the surgeon to determine the need for surgery
    C. Dressing changes
    D. Preoperative visits after the decision is made to operate

24. Modifier 78 is to be used when the physician needs to indicate

    A. another procedure performed during the postoperative period of the initial procedure
    B. a basic procedure performed by another physician had to be repeated
    C. a repeat procedure on the same day by the same physician
    D. a staged or related procedure or service by the same physician during the postoperative period of the original surgery

25. Which of the following can NOT be performed via laparoscope?

    A. Nephrectomy
    B. Cholecystectomy
    C. Appendectomy
    D. Craniotomy

Radiology

26. Which of the following radiological procedures views the interior of the body with x-rays and projects the image onto a television screen?   26.____

   A. Angiography
   B. Magnetic Resonance Imaging (MRI)
   C. Fluoroscopy
   D. Xeroradiography

27. The unlisted code used for cardiovascular procedures is   27.____

   A. 75960
   B. 76509
   C. 77799
   D. 78499

28. The movement of a body part away from the midline of the body is known as   28.____

   A. abduction
   B. extension
   C. adduction
   D. pronation

29. CPT code _____ denotes a procedure by which the cor- neal thickness is measured and used to diagnose and manage glaucoma.   29.____

   A. 76511
   B. 76514
   C. 76516
   D. 76519

Pathology & Laboratory

30. An arterial blood sample is drawn from a patient at three different intervals on the same day, and arterial blood gas testing is performed three times that same day. The procedural code for the ABG would be entered   30.____

   A. 82803-91
   B. 82803 x 3
   C. 82803, 82803-59, 82803-59
   D. 82803-59

31. Antibodies for hepatitis C, total and IgM are determined. The correct way to code for these procedures would be   31.____

   A. 86803
   B. 86803, 86803-59
   C. 86803, 86803-91
   D. 86803, 86709

32. Code for a urine lithium assay that is performed to determine a patient's compliance with a therapy program.

    A. 81001
    B. 81020
    C. 80101
    D. 80178

Medicine

33. Which of the following CPT codes is associated with primary care?

    A. 90918
    B. 92953
    C. 94010
    D. 96459

34. A Medicare patient comes to a physician's office for a prothrombin time (PT) test and the international normalized ratio (INR) test. The nurse determines the INR to be 3.7 and the target is 2-3. She notifies the physician, who adjusts the coumadin dosage but never sees the patient. The most appropriate code for this visit would be

    A. G0351, 86510
    B. 86510
    C. 99211, 00351
    D. 99211, 36415, 86510

35. For which of the following medical professionals is it appropriate to submit CPT's pharmalogic management code 90862?
    I. Family physicians
    II. Pediatricians
    III. Psychiatrists
    IV. Advanced practice psychiatric nurses

    A. I only
    B. I and II
    C. I, II and III
    D. I, II, III and IV

36. A patient receives an IM injection of RSV immune globulin in the physician's office. The coding for this service is

    A. 90378
    B. 90782
    C. G0351, 90378
    D. G0351

37. The purpose of tonometry is to

    A. track the movement of the eye as it follows moving objects
    B. measure intraocular pressure
    C. see into the fundus of the eye
    D. examine the angles of the eye

38. Which of the following modifiers is applicable to medicine?

    A. 22
    B. 25
    C. 26
    D. 51

HCPCS

39. Code for a routine venipuncture for specimen collection

    A. A0001
    B. 36415
    C. G0002
    D. 36416

40. During a session with a physical therapist, a patient received 24 minutes of neuromuscular re-education, followed by 23 minutes of therapeutic exercises to develop the strength, endurance, range of motion and flexibility of an injured leg. The correct coding is

    A. 97112, 97110
    B. 97112x2, 97110
    C. 97112, 97110x2
    D. 97110x3

41. The "J" codes in HCPCPS indicate

    A. all medications
    B. durable medical equipment
    C. medical and surgical supplies
    D. drugs other than oral drugs

Medical Tests & Devices

42. Liver function tests include
    I. Albumin
    II. Prothrombin time (PT
    III. Bilirubin
    IV. Serum protein electrophoresis

    A. I only
    B. I and III
    C. I, III and IV
    D. I, II, III and IV

43. A hematologic study is a test on the function and status of the

    A. endocrine system
    B. lymphatic system
    C. liver
    D. blood

Anatomy

44. The outer layer of the bone, which serves as an attachment point for tendons and ligaments, is the

   A. periosteum
   B. fibrous layer
   C. epiphysis
   D. osteoblast

45. The structure of the kidney that is the first to receive completely formed urine is the

   A. pyramid
   B. minor calyx
   C. renal capsule
   D. renal cortex

46. Each of the following is a function of insulin, EXCEPT the increase of

   A. glucose transport into cells
   B. the use of fats for energy
   C. the conversion of glucose to glycogen in liver and muscles
   D. transport of amino acids and fatty acids into cells for synthesis

CPT & HCPCS Level II Conventions

47. Unlisted procedure codes in CPT always end in

   A. 0 or 00
   B. 0000
   C. 9 or 99
   D. X or XX

48. According to the guidelines for using the CPT index, a coder should begin with the

   A. conditions
   B. abbreviations
   C. organ or anatomical site
   D. procedure or service

49. In the CPT manual, some procedural listings include a semicolon. The purpose of the semicolon is to

   A. divide the procedure into common and unique portions
   B. coordinate procedures with appropriate add-on or adjunct procedures
   C. indicate changed subsection guidelines
   D. indicate deleted CPT codes

50. Add-on procedures are always reported

   A. in conjunction with another HCPCS code
   B. in conjunction with another CPT code
   C. to prolong the global surgical period
   D. with modifier -51

KEY (CORRECT ANSWERS)

1. A	11. A	21. B	31. B	41. D
2. C	12. D	22. D	32. C	42. D
3. B	13. B	23. B	33. B	43. D
4. A	14. B	24. A	34. D	44. A
5. B	15. B	25. D	35. D	45. B
6. D	16. D	26. C	36. C	46. B
7. C	17. D	27. D	37. B	47. C
8. D	18. B	28. A	38. A	48. D
9. A	19. C	29. B	39. B	49. A
10. C	20. A	30. A	40. B	50. B

EXAMINATION SECTION
TEST 1

DIRECTIONS: Each question or incomplete statement is followed by several suggested answers or completions. Select the one that BEST answers the question or completes the statement. *PRINT THE LETTER OF THE CORRECT ANSWER IN THE SPACE AT THE RIGHT.*

Medical Terminology

1. Which of the following medical terms denotes a malignant cancerous tumor?   1.____

    A. myeloma
    B. melanoma
    C. lipoma
    D. papilloma

2. In medical terms, the root "enter" indicates the   2.____

    A. stomach
    B. spleen
    C. intestine
    D. integument

3. When a temporary opening in the voice box is wanted, the surgical procedure used is a   3.____

    A. laryngotomy
    B. laryngectomy
    C. laryngostomy
    D. laryngoscopy

ICD-9-CM

4. A patient has been diagnosed with primary osteoarthritis of both knees. What is the diagnosis code?   4.____

    A. 715.0
    B. 715.16L.715.16R
    C. 715.16
    D. 715.19

5. A patient was admitted secondary to a breakthrough convulsive seizure. Her medications were adjusted, and she did not have any further seizures while in the hospital. The appropriate diagnostic code for the seizure is   5.____

    A. 345.11
    B. 345.9
    C. 780.2
    D. 780.39

6. A patient in a nursing home has been diagnosed with diabetic neuropathy. There is no indication of the type of diabetes in the documentation. The correct code would be   6.____

A. 357.2, 250.6
B. 250.6
C. 357.2
D. 250.6, 357.2

7. Within the "malignant" section of the neoplasm table listed in the Alphabetic section of the ICD-9-CM, there are three available descriptions. Which of the following is NOT one of them?

   A. Primary
   B. Secondary
   C. Uncertain behavior
   D. In situ

8. A "late effect" is defined as a

   A. residual effect that follows the acute phase of an injury or illness
   B. condition that results as a complication from an implanted device or surgical procedure
   C. psychiatric symptoms that are always coded separately
   D. side effect due to a medication

9. When a patient is admitted for further observation, evaluation, or treatment less than 8 weeks after a myocardial infarction, a fifth digit code of _____ should be used to designate the episode of care

   A. 0
   B. 1
   C. 2
   D. 7

Evaluation & Management

10. A certified nursing specialist spends a 15-minute visit counseling an established patient with bipolar disorder on the necessity of complying with the medication regimen. The most appropriate E&M code for this encounter is

    A. 99203
    B. 99205
    C. 99213
    D. 99401

11. When a physician must direct emergency care via a two-way communication system for advanced life support, code _____ is used.

    A. 99287
    B. 99288
    C. 99289
    D. 99290

12. A patient is seeking a second opinion for his own physician's recommendation for surgical repair of a hernia. The consulting physician conducts a brief problem-focused history of present illness, and a problem-focused examination of the affected body area and organ system. The medical decision making was straightforward.
    The most appropriate E&M code for this visit is

    A. 99243
    B. 99271
    C. 99275
    D. 99282

13. In reference to E & M, the term "concurrent care" means that

    A. a patient is being treated for more than one condition at a time
    B. one or more physicians provided similar services on the same day
    C. a physician is providing ongoing review and revisions of the patient's care plan, which involves a multidisciplinary approach
    D. more than one surgeon participated in the same procedure

14. "Contributory factors" in E & M include each of the following, EXCEPT

    A. examination
    B. time
    C. coordination of care
    D. nature of the presenting problem

Anesthesia

15. An anesthesia code is followed by the HCPCS modifier G9. This means that the anesthesia service is

    A. provided by a certified nurse anesthetist (CRNA) with a physician's medical direction
    B. monitored anesthesia care (MAC) for a deep, complex, complicated, or markedly invasive surgical procedure
    C. monitored anesthesia care (MAC) for a patient who has a history of severe cardiopulmonary problems
    D. performed personally by the anesthesiologist

16. Which of the following anesthesia services is always considered part of the global surgical package, and is not billed separately?

    A. Conscious sedation
    B. Peripheral nerve block
    C. Field block
    D. General anesthesia

Surgery & Modifiers

17. A surgeon performs a 3-level laminectomy for resection of an intradural/extramedullary spinal cord tumor. The appropriate way to code this procedure is

A. 63281
B. 63281, 63281-51, 63281-51
C. 63281, 63281-59, 63281-59
D. 63281 x 3

18. Code a diagnostic laparoscopy.

    A. 50545
    B. 50544
    C. 49345
    D. 49320

19. Code for an excision of basal cell carcinoma, one third of the eyelid, with frozen section control of the margins.

    A. 67961
    B. 67966
    C. 66982
    D. 67999

20. During an office visit, an ophthalmologist performs a gonioscopy on both of a patient's eyes. What is the correct way to code this procedure?

    A. 92020-50
    B. 92020-LT, 92020-RT
    C. 92020 x 2
    D. 92020

21. When a vasotomy is performed,

    A. a vasectomy is reversed
    B. the vas deferens is sutured
    C. an opening is created in the vas deferens
    D. a new connection between the vas deferens and the epididymis is created

22. A repair of a femoral hernia (49550) is performed on January 5. The postoperative period designation for this procedure code is 90 days.
    On February 12, the same physician performs an appendectomy. The physician should report the appendectomy as

    A. 44950 (49550)
    B. 44950
    C. 44950-79
    D. 44950-59

23. A surgeon controls an anterior nasal hemorrhage through nasal endoscopy. The code for this procedure is

    A. 30901, 31235
    B. 31237, 31255
    C. 31238
    D. 30903

24. Anesthesia for an initial pericardiocentesis is begun at an ASC and the procedure has been started, but the physician terminates the procedure before it is completed. The procedure would

    A. not be coded
    B. be coded as 33010-52
    C. be coded as 33010-73
    D. be coded as 33010-74

Radiology

25. A physician performs a saline hysterosonogram in her office. The correct coding for this procedure is

    A. 58340, 76831
    B. 58340, 76830
    C. 76856
    D. 76831

26. Just prior to the single port stimulation of a liver tumor, the oncologist externally administers hyperthermia. The correct way to code the procedures would be

    A. 77280, 77600
    B. 77280, 77605
    C. 77260, 77605
    D. 77470, 77600

27. The radiological term that refers to views farthest away from the center, midline, or trunk is

    A. distal
    B. medial
    C. lateral
    D. proximal

28. In radiology, a "caudal" view is synonymous with

    A. inferior
    B. anterior
    C. ventral
    D. posterior

Pathology & Laboratory

29. A complete blood count (CBC) includes each of the following, EXCEPT

    A. hematocrit (HCT)
    B. mean corpuscular hemoglobin (MCH)
    C. partial thromboplastin time (PTT)
    D. differential screen (WBC)

30. Drug testing codes fall in the range of

    A. 80100-80103
    B. 80400-80440
    C. 82000-85999
    D. 86805-86849

31. A pathologist in the medical center's blood bank is asked to evaluate a written report on data that indicates the detection of a possible irregular cluster of blood antibodies. The code for this report would be

    A. 80500
    B. 80502
    C. 86077
    D. 88125

32. Which of the following modifiers is applicable to laboratory services?

    A. 51
    B. 58
    C. 74
    D. 91

Medicine

33. A newborn infant is seen at the office of a family medicine physician for a two-week well-child check. The infant is a new patient, but was seen earlier by the physician at the hospital after delivery. The appropriate code for this visit is

    A. 99381
    B. 99382
    C. 99391
    D. 99392

34. The range of codes that deals with cardiography is

    A. 92950-93278
    B. 93000-93350
    C. 93501-93562
    D. 93600-93660

35. Of the following procedures, which would be considered in CPT terms to be a "biopsy" rather than an "excision"?
    I. Partial removal of a lesion, with the intent to identify the lesion
    II. Complete removal of a lesion, with the intent to identify the lesion
    III. Partial removal of a lesion, with the intent to remove the lesion
    IV. Complete removal of a lesion, with the intent to remove the lesion

    A. I only
    B. I and II
    C. I and III
    D. I, II, III and IV

36. The most appropriate code for a combination vaccine injection given to a 12-year-old against diphtheria, tetanus, and pertussis (whooping cough) would be

    A. 90471, 90715
    B. 90471, 90700
    C. 90471, 90749
    D. 90471, G0351

37. In _____, air pressure in the ear canal is varied to test the condition and mobility of the ear drum.

    A. tympanometry
    B. audiometry
    C. myringotomy
    D. reflectometry

HCPCS

38. A diagnostic colonoscopy was begun, but it was found that the patient was inadequately prepped for the procedure, so the procedure was discontinued and no exam of the sigmoid was possible. The procedure should

    A. be billed as 45378
    B. be billed as 45378-73
    C. be billed as 45378-53
    D. not be billed at all

39. A patient is given an injection of 2.4 million units of penicillin G benthazine. The code for this is

    A. J0570 x 2
    B. J0580 x 2
    C. J0560
    D. J0580

40. Level III HCPCS codes are

    A. not billable to inpatient facilities
    B. numeric codes identical to CPT codes
    C. alpha-numeric codes beginning with A-V
    D. alpha-numeric codes beginning with W-Z

41. A 60-year-old established patient, during a visit to her physician's office, has a 1.7-cm benign skin lesion removed from her back. A surgical tray is used during the procedure. The correct procedural code for this visit is

    A. 11402
    B. 11421
    C. 11402, A4550
    D. 11421, A4550

Medical Tests & Devices

42. A stent is a medical device generally used to 42.____

    A. bypass a blocked artery
    B. protect the spinal cord
    C. keep a formerly or potentially blocked passageway open
    D. drain excess cerebrospinal fluid

43. What is the type of device that senses a person's heart rhythm during cardiac arrest and, 43.____
    in some cases, delivers an electric shock to get the heart beating again?

    A. Defibrillator
    B. Beta blocker
    C. Pacemaker
    D. Lead

    Anatomy

44. Cardiac muscles differ from other muscles in that they have 44.____

    A. fibers connected to one another at intercalated disks
    B. striations
    C. larger fibers than other striated muscles
    D. fewer mitochondria

45. The human skeleton is considered to have two divisions: the 45.____

    A. bony and cartilaginous
    B. compact and spongy
    C. axial and appendicular
    D. gross and fine

46. Blood cells are produced in the hemopoietic tissues, of which there are two types: 46.____

    A. red and yellow bone marrow
    B. red bone marrow and lymphatic tissue
    C. endocrine tissue and lymphatic tissue
    D. yellow bone marrow and lymphatic tissue

    CPT & HCPCS Level II Conventions

47. Which of the following CPT codes are considered to be exempt from modifier 51? 47.____

    A. Add-on codes
    B. Surgery codes
    C. Separate procedures
    D. Multiple procedures

48. When a coder uses modifier 51, the recommended practice is to 48.____

    A. include a report to ensure reimbursement
    B. use it on all procedures for that section
    C. list the highest charge procedure first
    D. use the RT or LT identifier as appropriate without a modifier

49. Which of the following is NOT an appendix found at the back of the CPT manual? 49.____

    A. Update to short descriptors
    B. Clinical examples of surgery codes
    C. Clinical examples of evaluation & management codes
    D. Summary of codes added, deleted, or revised

50. A coder, in a physician's documentation, comes across a procedure that is not listed in the CPT manual. The coder's FIRST step should be to 50.____

    A. find the procedural code that most closely approximates the one documented
    B. code with the appropriate "unlisted procedure" CPT Level I code
    C. look for an appropriate Category III code
    D. contact the physician for clarification

KEY (CORRECT ANSWERS)

1. A	11. B	21. C	31. C	41. C
2. C	12. B	22. C	32. D	42. C
3. A	13. B	23. C	33. C	43. A
4. C	14. A	24. D	34. B	44. A
5. D	15. C	25. A	35. B	45. C
6. D	16. C	26. A	36. A	46. B
7. C	17. A	27. A	37. A	47. A
8. A	18. D	28. A	38. C	48. C
9. C	19. C	29. C	39. D	49. B
10. C	20. D	30. A	40. D	50. C

TEST 2

DIRECTIONS: Each question or incomplete statement is followed by several suggested answers or completions. Select the one that BEST answers the question or completes the statement. *PRINT THE LETTER OF THE CORRECT ANSWER IN THE SPACE AT THE RIGHT.*

Medical Terminology

1. The duodenum is   1.____

    A. a hollow jointed tube that connects the stomach to the intestine
    B. the central of the three divisions of the small intestine
    C. a pouch connected to the large intestine between the ileum and the colon
    D. the part of the digestive system immediately behind the mouth and in front of the esophagus

2. If an organ or tissue is afflicted with calculi, it may be necessary to surgically crush the   2.____
   calculi so they may be passed. The medical term describing this procedure is

    A. calculocentesis
    B. lithotripsy
    C. lithotomy
    D. lithiasis

3. The endometrium is the   3.____

    A. uterine membrane that is thickened in preparation for fertilization, and into which a fertilized egg is implanted
    B. portion of the lower uterus where the uterus joins with the top end of the vagina
    C. temporary) organ present only in women during pregnancy
    D. layer of smooth muscle forming the uterine wall

4. Anticholinergics are a category of drugs that work against   4.____

    A. irregular heartbeats
    B. parasympathetic nerve impulses
    C. infective agents
    D. toxins

ICD-9-CM

5. A physician has diagnosed a patient with hypertensive renal sclerosis, without kidney   5.____
   failure. Though the physician has not specified whether the hypertension is benign or
   malignant, the coder knows from the history that it is a serious and life-threatening case.
   The coder should use the diagnostic code

    A. 401.9,586
    B. 403.00
    C. 403.10
    D. 403.9

6. A two-year-old patient is taken to a physician who observes the presence of ptosis in one eyelid, heterochromia and the absence of a horizontal eyelid crease in the ptotic eye. He diagnoses the child with Horner's syndrome of congenital origin. The correct diagnosis code for this visit is

   A. 743.61, 743.46, 337.9
   B. 337.9, 743,46
   C. 446.5
   D. 337.9

7. Code for encephalitis attributable to infectious mononucleosis.

   A. 323.4, 075
   B. 323.2, 075
   C. 323.0, 078.3
   D. 323.0, 075

8. Code for a history of a CVA with no residuals.

   A. 437.0
   B. 437.9
   C. VI 2.49
   D. V 12.59

9. A patient who has an inconclusive HIV test result should be coded

   A. V08
   B. 759.71
   C. 042.0
   D. 042.9

10. For which of the following purposes would an M code be appropriate?

    A. Describing the cell type of a neoplasm
    B. Providing a secondary diagnosis to provide further information
    C. Identifying the cause of an injury
    D. Identifying the etiology of a disease

Evaluation & Management

11. What range of codes is used to report Evaluation and Management (E/M) services provided within the emergency department of a hospital?

    A. 99201-99215
    B. 99271-99275
    C. 99281-99285
    D. 99291-99292

12. In his office, a physician meets a 30-year-old new patient who complains of a lesion on his neck. The physician conducts and documents an expanded problem-focused history of the presenting problem, followed by an expanded examination of the back, chest, abdomen, and neck for similar lesions. The physician's assessment reveals low risk of complications, and limited management options for low-complexity decision making. No testing is required.
The most appropriate E&M code for this visit is

    A. 99201
    B. 99202
    C. 99210
    D. 99213

13. In the Evaluation and Management section of CPT, there are 5 levels of consulting codes. Level 2 denotes

    A. detailed history and exam, low complexity decision
    B. problem-focused history and exam, straightforward decision
    C. comprehensive history and exam, moderate complexity decision
    D. expanded problem-focused history and exam, straightforward decision

14. The three key E&M components are

    A. nature of the presenting problem, coordination of care, medical decision making
    B. history, examination, medical decision making
    C. coordination of care, medical decision making, time
    D. examination, nature of the presenting problem, time

Anesthesia

15. What range of codes is used to represent general anesthesia?

    A. 00100-01953
    B. 01905-01933
    C. 01968-01969
    D. 01990-01999

16. Prior to performing an iridectomy, a surgeon administers the necessary anesthesia. The appropriate anesthesia code is

    A. 00140
    B. 00142
    C. 00144
    D. 00147

17. Which of the following modifiers is NOT applicable to anesthesia?

    A. 22
    B. 32
    C. 47
    D. 55

Surgery & Modifiers

18. A surgeon shortens the superior oblique muscle in one eye of a patient with strabismus, and performs a suture on the revised muscle. The code for this procedure is

    A. 67318
    B. 67318, 67335
    C. 67318, 67334
    D. 67314, 67334

19. Which of the following is NOT a CPT code in the integumentary section that covers surgical trays?

    A. 19110
    B. 19120
    C. 19125
    D. 19127

20. In the emergency room, a hematoma is excised and drained in a patient's shoulder and the surgeon explores the penetrating wound in the upper arm. The most appropriate coding for this procedure would be

    A. 23030
    B. 23030, 20103-59
    C. 23030, 20103
    D. 20103

21. A patient undergoes open treatment of hip fracture, with interior fixation. Later, after the patient develops severe stomach pain, she returns to the operating room for an appendectomy. The appropriate coding for these procedures is

    A. 27226, 44950
    B. 27226, 44950-59
    C. 27226, 44950-78
    D. 27226, 44950-79

22. Code for a radical unilateral cervical lymphadenectomy.

    A. 38720
    B. 38760
    C. 38765
    D. 38770

23. A surgeon attempts to correct for a patient's sleep apnea by performing a laser uvulopalatopharyngoplasty (UPPP). The correct coding for this procedure would be

    A. 21206
    B. 42145, 21198
    C. 42145
    D. 42160

24. When "considerably more than is customary" is performed during a given procedure, which modifier is used?

A. 21
B. 22
C. 24
D. 52

25. Which of the following modifiers has been deleted? 25.____

    A. 20
    B. 22
    C. 25
    D. 50

Radiology

26. A radiologic view that is aligned left to right and divides the body into front and back components, viewed from front to back, is 26.____

    A. sagittal
    B. ventral
    C. coronal
    D. axial

27. Code for radiologic examination; both knees, standing, anteroposterior 27.____

    A. 73540
    B. 73550
    C. 73564
    D. 73565

28. Code for a CT angiography of the upper extremity, with contrast medium. 28.____

    A. 73200
    B. 73206
    C. 73218
    D. 73219

29. Code for radiologic examination of the mastoids, four per side. 29.____

    A. 70120
    B. 70130
    C. 70134
    D. 70140

Pathology & Laboratory

30. In most cases, coded reports for blood tests are accompanied by the code _____, which indicates the collection of venous blood by venous puncture. 30.____

    A. G0005
    B. 36415
    C. 36416
    D. 36420

31. Pap smears, needle aspirations, and chromosomal tests are included in CPT code range

    A. 86000-86849
    B. 87001-87999
    C. 88104-88299
    D. 88300-88309

32. The _____ is a test that reveals the amount of red blood cells in whole blood

    A. mean corpuscular hemoglobin (MCH)
    B. platelet count
    C. differential screen
    D. hematocrit (HTC)

Medicine

33. A 9-year-old girl is brought into the physician's office unexpectedly by her mother on a very busy clinic day. She is wheezing. She has no known history of asthma but frequently gets like this while playing basketball. The physician takes a history and performs an exam. She then performs a spirometry and checks oximetry, and ends by giving the girl a nebulizer treatment with 3 mg of albuterol solution.
The most appropriate coding for this visit would be

    A. 99058, 94010, 94670, 94640
    B. 99058, 94010, 94670, 94640, J7616
    C. 99214, 99058, 94010, 94670, 94640, J7616
    D. 99214, 99058-25, 94010, 94670, 94640, J7611

34. A patient has a metacarpal joint aspirated and injected on the same date in a family physician's office. The correct code for these procedures would be

    A. 20600
    B. 20600, 20600-59
    C. 20600, 20600
    D. 20605

35. Code for a routine ECG, tracing only, without interpretation or report.

    A. 93000
    B. 93005
    C. 93010
    D. 93012

36. Another term for "treatment method" is

    A. evaluation
    B. modality
    C. intervention
    D. diagnosis

37. The code for an IM injection of an antibiotic agent is

    A. 90782
    B. 90783
    C. 90784
    D. 90788

38. A 3-year-old girl visits the emergency room after ingesting lead. She is treated with gastric lavage. The code for this procedure is

    A. 43752
    B. 43242
    C. 91105
    D. 43752, 91105

HCPCS

39. A patient has a rigid knee orthosis fabricated for him, without a knee joint. The code for this is

    A. L1815
    B. L1832
    C. L1834
    D. L1845

40. A colonoscopy was advanced as far as the splenic flexion, but was then discontinued due to the patient's discomfort. The procedure should

    A. be billed as 45378
    B. be billed as 45378-73
    C. be billed as 45378-53
    D. not be billed at all

Medical Tests & Devices

41. Which of the following is a device that may be used to relieve pressure on the brain?

    A. Catheter
    B. Stent
    C. Reservoir
    D. Shunt

42. Which of the following tests is LEAST likely to be used to evaluate a patient's epilepsy? patient?

    A. EEG
    B. Cerebral arteriogram
    C. CT scan
    D. MRI

Anatomy

43. The basic structural and functional unit of the kidney is the   43.____

    A. renal capsule
    B. nephron
    C. calyx
    D. renal cortex

44. Of the connective tissue membranes that cover the brain, the outermost is the   44.____

    A. dura mater
    B. pia mater
    C. arachnoid membrane
    D. cerebral cortex

45. Which of the following arteries does NOT supply blood to the brain?   45.____

    A. internal carotid
    B. external carotid
    C. maxillary
    D. basilar

46. The antibody that is produced FIRST during an infection is   46.____

    A. IgA
    B. IgE
    C. IgG
    D. IgM

CPT & HCPCS Level II Conventions

47. Level II HCPCS modifiers include each of the following, EXCEPT   47.____

    A. -VP
    B. -57
    C. -AA
    D. -TI

48. For CPT code 42820, the "medical necessity" criterion would be met by linking it with the ICD-9-CM code   48.____

    A. 032.0
    B. 474.02
    C. 474.2
    D. 487.1

49. A coder is reporting the excision of a lesion that has been documented as having dimensions of 4 cm x 2 cm x 1.5 cm. The coder should report the lesion as having a dimension of _____ cm.   49.____

    A. 2.5 cm
    B. 4 cm
    C. 8 cm^2
    D. 12 cm^3

50. The Level II modifiers that specify digits on each foot are 50.____
    A. El to E4
    B. TA to T9
    C. FA to F9
    D. GA to GY

KEY (CORRECT ANSWERS)

1. A	11. C	21. D	31. C	41. D
2. B	12. B	22. A	32. D	42. B
3. A	13. D	23. D	33. C	43. B
4. B	14. B	24. B	34. A	44. A
5. D	15. A	25. A	35. B	45. C
6. D	16. D	26. C	36. B	46. D
7. D	17. D	27. D	37. D	47. B
8. D	18. C	28. B	38. C	48. B
9. B	19. D	29. B	39. C	49. B
10. A	20. B	30. B	40. A	50. B

EXAMINATION SECTION
TEST 1

DIRECTIONS: Each question or incomplete statement is followed by several suggested answers or completions. Select the one that BEST answers the question or completes the statement. *PRINT THE LETTER OF THE CORRECT ANSWER IN THE SPACE AT THE RIGHT.*

Medical Terminology

1. When a physician treats a fracture with a splint or cast, the method of treatment is described as

    A. closed manipulation
    B. internal fixation
    C. external fixation
    D. open stasis

2. An encephalocele is a

    A. tumor of the lymph
    B. brain tumor
    C. softened portion of brain tissue
    D. protrusion of brain tissue through a cranial fissure

3. When a physician treats a fracture with a splint or cast, the method of treatment is described as

    A. closed manipulation
    B. internal fixation
    C. external fixation
    D. open stasis

4. In medical terms, the root "stomat" indicates the

    A. stomach
    B. esophagus
    C. ear
    D. mouth

5. The medical abbreviation ESRD stands for

    A. endoesophageal rupture
    B. extrasensory ruminative disorder
    C. enterostatic rheumatic disease
    D. end-stage renal disease

6. The medical term for an incision into the duodenum is

    A. duodenotomy
    B. duodenectomy
    C. duodenoplasty
    D. duodenostomy

7. The medical term "phrenogastric" would be used to describe something pertaining to the   7._____

   A. liver and stomach
   B. kidney and intestine
   C. diaphragm and stomach
   D. head and abdomen

8. In medical terms, the root "acr(o)" is used to refer to the   8._____

   A. lower jaw
   B. extremities
   C. digits
   D. lower back

9. In a medical record, the abbreviation Sx means   9._____

   A. simulation
   B. blood glucose
   C. symptoms
   D. sepsis

ICD-9-CM

10. A patient was admitted to the emergency room. He reported a sudden hearing loss in his left ear, over a period of several hours, which was accompanied by a loud sound in his left ear. He can now barely hear out of his left ear. The physician's diagnosis is sudden sensorineural deafness. The diagnosis code is   10._____

    A. 388.12
    B. 306.7
    C. 388.2
    D. 389.1

11. A patient is admitted to the hospital with burns over 40% of his body. 15% of his body surface has third-degree burns. The correct diagnostic code is   11._____

    A. 948.1
    B. 948.14
    C. 948.4
    D. 948.41

12. A patient has IDDM, uncontrolled, with a polyneuropathy. What is the correct code for this?   12._____

    A. 250.6, 357.2
    B. 250.63, 357.2
    C. 357.2, 250.6
    D. 250.63

13. A pregnant woman is HIV-positive but asymptomatic. The most accurate diagnostic code for her is   13._____

    A. 647.60,
    B. 647.60, V08

C. V08.647.60
D. 042.9

14. A hypertensive patient undergoes a scan that reveals an unruptured cerebral aneurysm that is a direct result of the hypertension. The physician's diagnosis reads only "hypertensive cerebrovascular disease, nonruptured aneurysm, subdural." The diagnostic code for this is

    A. 401.9, 432.1
    B. 401.1, 432.1
    C. 437.3, 401.9
    D. 437.3, 401.1

15. A patient's diagnosis includes both acute renal failure with tubular necrosis and chronic (malignant) hypertensive renal failure. The coder should

    A. code both in the following order: 404.02, 584.5
    B. code both in the following order: 584.5, 404.02
    C. code only 404.04
    D. code only 584.5

16. Which of the following statements is/are TRUE of ICD-9-CM code 650, Normal Delivery?
    I. Code 650 is used in cases when a woman is admitted for a full-term normal delivery and delivers a single, healthy infant without any complications antepartum, during delivery, or post-partum.
    II. The only outcome code appropriate for use with code 650 is V27.0.
    III. Code 650 is usually, but not always, the principal diagnosis.
    IV. 650 may NOT be used if the patient had complications at any point in her pregnancy.

    A. I only
    B. I and II
    C. I, II and III
    D. I, II, III and IV

17. For coding purposes, the "postpartum" period begins immediately after delivery and continues for _____ weeks following delivery.

    A. 4
    B. 6
    C. 8
    D. 12

Payment Methodologies

18. When CMS electronically forwards secondary claim information, a(n) _____ claim is said to have occurred.

    A. dirty
    B. vapor
    C. crossover
    D. duplicate

19. On CMS 1500, the treating intern's name and license number would be entered in box   19.____

    A. 10d
    B. 17 and 17a
    C. 24k
    D. 33

20. In FL 22 of CMS 1450, a routine patient discharge is coded   20.____

    A. 01
    B. 07
    C. 10
    D. 20

21. Condition codes are   21.____

    A. used to administer primary or secondary insurance
    B. not required for Medicare claims
    C. used to denote the level of ambulatory patient classification (APC)
    D. used to determine eligibility and benefits

22. Which of the following would be included in the facility fee charge?   22.____

    A. Lease of durable medical equipment
    B. Screening mammography
    C. Blood products and services
    D. Surgically implanted prosthetics

23. Of the following facilities, the one LEAST likely to be reimbursed under the Ambulatory Payment Classification (APC) system would be a   23.____

    A. hospital participating in Medicare
    B. critical access hospital (CAH) paid at cost
    C. small rural hospital
    D. community mental health center

24. Procedure codes with a status modifier _____ are considered "inpatient only procedures."   24.____

    A. A
    B. C
    C. G
    D. P

25. A hospital's chargemaster, or charge description master (CDM), typically does NOT include   25.____

    A. an inventory listing
    B. ICD-9-CM codes
    C. revenue codes
    D. HCPCS codes

General CPT

26. Code for an intradermal tuberculosis skin test.

    A. 86580
    B. Y2012
    C. 86585
    D. 0010T

27. When the main focus of a visit is to recommend major surgery to be performed that day or the next day, modifier _____ is used.

    A. 25
    B. 53
    C. 57
    D. 71

28. A patient has had a dystrophic nail trimmed. The code for this procedure is

    A. 11719
    B. 11720
    C. 11721
    D. G0127

29. Modifier 50 is used when a procedure

    A. involves more than one organ system
    B. is performed twice in the same location
    C. is performed on both the right and left sides of the body
    D. is aborted before it is completed

30. Which of the following is "0-day" CPT code?

    A. 17106
    B. 10060
    C. 17260
    D. 11040

31. Code for nonobstetrical repair of the cervix, using cerclage.

    A. 57700
    B. 57710
    C. 58145
    D. 58270

32. The CPT modifier for "repeat clinical diagnostic laboratory service" is

    A. 59
    B. 79
    C. 80
    D. 91

33. A surgeon is seeing a patient who has been referred to him by a colleague who wants to determine whether one of her established patients, a 76-year-old male, is able to withstand the general anesthesia required to remove a cancerous colon tumor.

The surgeon evaluates the patient in his office, performing a history and physical examination, and pays special attention to his cardiovascular system because he has a history of aortic stenosis. The surgeon also orders and perform a routine electrocardiogram (ECG) and write a report after interpreting the findings.

Based on the information above, the most appropriate coding for this visit would be

- A. 99245
- B. 99241, 93000 (V72.81)
- C. 99241 (V72.81), 93000 (V72.81), 153.9, 424.1
- D. 99245 (V72.81), 93000 (V72.81), 153.2, 423.9

34. An established patient visits the outpatient clinic suffering from exhaustion and dehydration. The physician orders an infusion of dextrose 5% (D5W), with electrolyte supplement. The patient was infused for three hours.
The most appropriate code for this visit is

- A. G0345, G0346 x 2, 276.6
- B. G0345x3, 276.6
- C. G0347, G0348 x 2, 276.6
- D. G0347 x 3, 276.6

35. A physician performs a percutaneous transluminal coronary angioplasty (PTCA) and places a stent in the right coronary artery. The procedure is monitored fluoroscopically. The correct way to code for this procedure is

- A. 92980, 92981
- B. 93508, 92978
- C. 92980, 92978
- D. 92980

Surgical Procedures

36. **_Operative Report_**
Preoperative Diagnosis: Vpattern esotropia with high accommodative convergence/ accommodation ratio (AC/A), OU.

Operation:
1. Inferior oblique recessions, OU (14.0 mm).
2. Left medial rectus recession 7.0 mm with posterior fixation suture.
3. Right medial rectus recession 5.0 mm.

Postoperative Diagnosis: *Vpattern esotropia with high accommodative convergence/accommodation ratio (AC/ A), OU.*

Indications: *Patient is a 43-year-old male with a history of right esotropia and strabismus surgery at a very young age (medial rectus recession) and dense amblyopia of the right eye.*

Operative Course: *... Forced auctions were performed which revealed a mild degree of tightness of the right medial rectus muscle. A lid speculum was placed. Attention was directed first toward the re-recession of the right medial rectus muscle. The eye was rotated into an abducted position, and a partial nasal limbal peritomy was fashioned using Westcott scissors.*

Careful dissection was carried out to remove scar tissue anterior and overlying the recessed medial rectus muscle .... Next, a single double-armed 6-0 Dexon suture was woven through the width of the muscle with blocking bites in the center and at the superior and inferior poles. The muscle was then disinserted using Aebli scissors. The suture needles were then brought back forward through the original muscle insertion in a crossed sword fashion and then tied together using a cinch knot. The cinch was placed at a position such that the muscle hung back 11.5 mm from the limbus. This arrangement was performed to allow adjustment of the suture the following morning based upon his postoperative ocular alignment measurements.

Next, the 6-0 plain gut sutures that were preplaced through the anterior corners of the conjunctival limbal peritomy were brought back through the limbus and tied in a loop. This allowed sagging of the conjunctiva to facilitate adjustment the following day.

Attention was then directed toward the right superior rectus muscle where a recession of 4.0 mm was performed... The position of the recess of the superior rectus muscle was then reexamined and deemed to be secure and in good position.

36. Based on the excerpted report on the preceding page, the most appropriate coding for this procedure would be

    A. 67314-50, 67334-LT, 67311-RT
    B. 67314, 67315, 67334-LT, 67311-RT
    C. 67314, 67334-50
    D. 67314, 67334, 67311

37. A patient presents to an orthopedic surgeon with a large mass on the back of her leg. The physician performs a biopsy of the mass, down to the muscle. The correct CPT code for this procedure is

    A. 11100
    B. 27323
    C. 27614
    D. 27618

38. Which of the following is included in the payment amount for a global surgery?

    A. Removal of cutaneous sutures
    B. Treatment for postoperative complications that requires a return trip to the operating room
    C. Evaluation & management service on the same day as an endoscopy
    D. Immunotherapy management for an organ transplant

39. A surgeon performs a posterolateral fusion of vertebrae T-6 to T-12. The clearest and most appropriate way of reporting this procedure is

    A. 22610, 22614-50 x 5
    B. 22610
    C. 22610, 22614x5
    D. 22614 x 6

40. A physician uses a #25 gauge needle and injects 0.1 cc of lidocaine to release trigger in two areas of the right trapezius, two areas of the right splenis capitis, two areas of the splenis cervicus, and two areas of the right sternocleidomastoid. The most appropriate code for this procedure is

    A. 20552, 20552-51
    B. 20553
    C. 20553, 20553-51
    D. 20553 x 2

41. "-Centesis" procedures are grouped in the CPT surgical codes for

    A. introduction or removal
    B. excision/debridement
    C. repair/reconstruction/revision
    D. incision

42. A 45-year-old woman has a Pap smear that shows a high-grade squa-mous intraepithelial lesion. Three years ago she had a radical hysterectomy for Stage 1B squamous cell carcinoma of the cervix. Acetic acid is applied to the entire vagina, which is then evaluated with the colposcope at several magnifications. A suspicious lesion is noted at the vaginal cuff and a second area in the mid-vagina. Both areas are injected with local anesthetic; biopsies are taken; and bleeding is controlled with silver nitrate.

    The appropriate CPT code for the procedure is
    A. 56821
    B. 57100
    C. 57421
    D. 57455

43. A hammertoe correction to both big toes in the same operative session would be coded

    A. 28285-TA, 28285-T5
    B. 28285-T1, 28285-T6
    C. 28285-LT, 28285-RT
    D. 28285-50

44. After a failed laser procedure was performed on an iris for glaucoma, a trabeculectomy ab externo is performed. The code for this procedure would be

    A. 66165
    B. 66170
    C. 66172
    D. 66999

45. A patient reports to his physician's office for a diagnostic colonoscopy. The scope is inserted, but the procedure is discontinued after the scope fails to pass the splenic flexure. The procedure

    A. should not be coded
    B. should be coded 45378-52
    C. should be coded 45378-73
    D. should be coded 45379

46. Mrs. Roberts, a 72-year-old established patient of Dr. Smithers, came to the office for her pre-op visit on September 7. She was initially seen on August 31 for complaints of increasing vaginal pressure and discomfort, bladder pressure, and urinary frequency. She was noted to have significant protrusion beyond the introitus as well as cystocele and rectocele. After a discussion of management options, Mrs. Roberts elected to have a vaginal hysterectomy in addition to the primary repair procedures. Surgery was scheduled for 2 weeks later.

    At the pre-op visit Dr. Smithers discussed in detail with Mrs. Roberts the risks, benefits, and alternatives to the planned surgical procedures. The patient voiced understanding and gave informed consent.

    After appropriate prepping and draping, Dr. Smithers performed a vaginal hysterectomy. The bowel was retracted and packed and the vaginal apex was suspended to the iliococcygeus ligaments. Dr. Smithers closed the vaginal vault with interrupted sutures.

    Smithers then tended to the anteroposterior repair. The anterior repair was completed without difficulty. Because the native tissues in the posterior compartment were found to be too weak to provide support alone, the decision was made to insert a mesh graft for the posterior repair.

    A catheter was placed and left in for bladder drainage. Mrs. Roberts was taken to the recovery room in stable condition.

    What are the correct codes to report the surgical services?

    A. 58260 x2, 57282
    B. 58260, 57260-51, 57282-51, 57267
    C. 58260-51, 57260-51, 57282-51, 57267-51
    D. 57260, 58260-51, 57282-51, 57267

46.____

Miscellaneous

47. Postural hypotension, reduced skin turgor, and lethargy may all indicate

    A. appendicitis
    B. dehydration
    C. septicemia
    D. renal failure

47.____

48. A new patient visits an ophthalmologist's hospital clinic. The ophthalmologist performs an intermediate evaluation which includes a history, external examination of the pupils, iris, cornea, and conjuctiva; an ophthalmoscopic examination of the lens, anterior chamber, retina, and optic disk; and a general medical observation. The most appropriate medicine code for this service would be

    A. 92002
    B. 92004
    C. 92014
    D. 99202

48.____

49. At a psychiatric clinic, a patient receives 30 minutes of crisis intervention services. This should be coded

　　A. H2017
　　B. H2017 x 2
　　C. H2011
　　D. H2011x2

49.____

50. Code for a blood test to detect the serum level of creatine phosphoki-nase (CPK).

　　A. 82550
　　B. 82552
　　C. 82550, 82552
　　D. 82555

50.____

KEY (CORRECT ANSWERS)

1. A	11. D	21. A	31. A	41. D
2. D	12. B	22. C	32. D	42. C
3. A	13. B	23. B	33. C	43. A
4. D	14. C	24. B	34. A	44. B
5. D	15. B	25. D	35. C	45. C
6. A	16. B	26. A	36. A	46. B
7. C	17. B	27. B	37. C	47. B
8. B	18. C	28. D	38. A	48. A
9. C	19. C	29. C	39. C	49. D
10. D	20. A	30. D	40. B	50. A

TEST 2

DIRECTIONS: Each question or incomplete statement is followed by several suggested answers or completions. Select the one that BEST answers the question or completes the statement. *PRINT THE LETTER OF THE CORRECT ANSWER IN THE SPACE AT THE RIGHT.*

Medical Terminology

1. The medical term for the destruction or breaking down of blood vessels is   1.____

    A. angioma
    B. arteriosclerosis
    C. hemarthrosis
    D. angiolysis

2. Hyperplasia is a medical term describing   2.____

    A. the defective formation of the spinal cord
    B. the overdevelopment of an organ
    C. progressive degeneration
    D. an unsustainably rapid rate of cellular division

3. In medical terms, which of the following is a prefix that indicates an object is livid or purplish in color?   3.____

    A. bili-
    B. peli-
    C. ferro-
    D. cyan(o)-

4. A condition of an organ or tissue involving the formation of pus often has the suffix   4.____

    A. -pyelitis
    B. -sepsis
    C. -pyosis
    D. -tresia

5. In medical terms, a nullipara is a(n)   5.____

    A. miscarriage
    B. woman who has never given birth
    C. blighted ovum
    D. aborted fetus

6. On a medical record, the abbreviation "ac" means   6.____

    A. after consultation
    B. antechamber
    C. before meals
    D. nothing by mouth

57

7. In medical terms, each of the following is an adjective suffix that means "pertaining to" or "relating to," EXCEPT

   A. -ac
   B. -ism
   C. -eal
   D. -ary

8. The mitral, or bicuspid valve is

   A. in the right side of the heart and prevents blood from flowing back into the atrium
   B. in the left side of the heart and prevents blood from flowing back into the atrium
   C. between the left ventricle and the aorta and prevents blood from flowing back into the heart from the aorta
   D. part of the pulmonary artery and prevents blood from flowing back into the right ventricle

9. The medical term for the excision of a rib or ribs is

   A. pleurectomy
   B. chondrectomy
   C. costectomy
   D. chondroplasty

ICD-9-CM

10. A patient is admitted to the emergency room after suffering for several days from spiking fevers and chills, rapid breathing, and a rapid heart rate. Shortly after admission, the patient displays several signs of shock: hypothermia, confusion, and falling blood pressure. After a series of tests and a blood culture, the physician issues a diagnosis of generalized sepsis with shock. The correct diagnostic code is

    A. 038.9, 785.59
    B. 038.9
    C. 999.3
    D. 785.59

11. A patient is suffering from acute pain in his right knee. Upon examination, it is determined that he is suffering from secondary osteoarthritis, which is attributable to a sprain injury he received years ago while playing football. What is the correct ICD-9-CM code(s) that should be reported for this encounter?

    A. 715.16, 905.7
    B. 715.2, E929.3
    C. 715.25, 905.7
    D. 715.26, 905.7, E929.3

12. A patient has been diagnosed with uncontrolled Type II diabetes, with renal manifestations. What is the correct code for this?

    A. 250.42; 581.81
    B. 250.40; 581.1
    C. 250.41
    D. 250

13. Code for Parkinson's disease secondary to haloperidol (Haldol) prescribed for chronic undifferentiated schizophrenia. 13._____

    A. 332.0, E939.2
    B. 332.1, E939.2, 295.62
    C. 332.1, E939.2,
    D. 332.1, E939.2, 295.02

14. A young male patient, while he is asymptomatic, has requested an AIDS screening test. The reason for his request, he says, is that he has frequently engaged in unprotected sex with a number of partners. He is given the test, but before the physician sends him to the laboratory, she counsels him about the links between his behaviors and transmission of HIV. The appropriate code for this encounter is 14._____

    A. V73.8
    B. V73.89, V65.44
    C. V73.89, V69.8, V65.44
    D. V65.44, V08

15. For coding purposes, an excisional debridement of an infected wound that is performed by a physician would be coded 15._____

    A. 86.22
    B. 86.28
    C. 85.69
    D. 93.57

16. Code for contractures of the right and left wrist due to a previous stroke. 16._____

    A. 718.43, 438.89
    B. 438.89, 718.43
    C. 438.89
    D. 718.44, 438.89

17. When less than 10 percent of the body surface has been involved in a third-degree burn, a fifth digit of _____ should be used. 17._____

    A. 0
    B. 1
    C. 5
    D. 9

Payment Methodologies

18. The order in which procedures are listed on CMS 1450 can affect 18._____

    A. the amount of reimbursement
    B. the likelihood of an OIG audit
    C. the length of time it takes for the claim to be paid
    D. none of the above

19. Health care services for the uniformed services and their dependents are provided by

    A. DEERS
    B. Veterans Affairs
    C. Medicare
    D. TRICARE

20. A patient who undergoes a same-day surgical procedure

    A. is always admitted to observation overnight
    B. may require observation overnight based on the physician's orders
    C. may also require observation services if a complication from the procedures requires monitoring beyond the usual 4-6 hour period
    D. is never admitted to require observation overnight

21. For an outpatient facility, a "high level" new patient encounter would include each of the following, EXCEPT

    A. routine or extensive tests
    B. routine nursing assessment
    C. vitals
    D. sample medications

22. Partial hospitalization claims are identified by the presence of condition code _____ on the claim.

    A. G3
    B. 09
    C. 41
    D. 44

23. FL 20 of CMS 1450 is coded "3." This means that the source of admission was a(n)

    A. emergency room admission
    B. HMO referral
    C. transfer from another hospital
    D. physician referral

24. A procedure code with the status indicator "P" indicates a(n)

    A. partial hospitalization
    B. clinic or emergency department visit
    C. ancillary service
    D. influenza or pneumococcal pneumonia vaccine

25. Which of the following statements about revenue codes is FALSE?

    A. They are always listed in ascending numerical order.
    B. They identify whether services were inpatient or outpatient.
    C. They are used on CMS 1450, but not CMS 1500.
    D. They validate assigned HCPCS codes.

General CPT

26. Which of the following CPT codes involves the hypodermis?

    A. 11040
    B. 11041
    C. 11043
    D. 11045

27. Which of the following procedural codes has been done incorrectly?

    A. 99201-21
    B. 99205-21
    C. 99215-21
    D. 99245-21

28. The correct way to report the intralesional administration of chemotherapy in two lesions is

    A. 96405 x 1 unit
    B. 96405 x 2 units
    C. G0353
    D. G0345 x 1 unit, G0345 x 1 unit

29. A patient has an open head injury and a contra-coup subdural hemato-ma. The surgeon performs a craniectomy for the open head injury and a burr hole drainage on the opposite side of the subdural hematoma. To correctly code for these two procedures, the coder should report

    A. 61304
    B. 61304, 61154-59
    C. 61304, 61154
    D. 61154, 61304-59

30. Descriptive components for emergency department levels of E & M service include each of the following, EXCEPT

    A. coordination of care
    B. time
    C. history
    D. nature of the presenting problem

31. Routine venipuncture is found in the _____ codes of CPT.

    A. surgery
    B. evaluation and management
    C. medical services
    D. pathology and laboratory

32. Category III CPT codes

    A. end with the letter F
    B. end with the letter T
    C. begin with the letter G
    D. end with the letters QW

33. Modifier 24 should ALWAYS be used with _____ codes.

    A. Surgical
    B. E&M
    C. Radiology
    D. Anesthesia

34. Code for kyphoplasty of the vertebral body, for treatment of a compression fracture.

    A. 22025
    B. 22315
    C. 22899
    D. 76012-26

35. Code for a simple pulmonary stress test.

    A. 94011
    B. 94620
    C. 94621
    D. 94680

Surgical Procedures

36. A 68-year-old man with a history of lung cancer that had been previously treated with radiation therapy has been determined to have a radiation-induced benign stricture of his mid-thoracic esophagus. The patient was taken to the endoscopy suite, and a video endoscope was advanced via the mouth into the esophagus to the level of the stricture. The degree of stenosis prevented passage of the scope beyond the stricture. A through-the-scope balloon dilator was passed through the endoscope and positioned across the stricture, which was then dilated to 11 mm. Then the balloon dilator was then withdrawn. In order to prevent another stricture formation at the site of previous scarring, a sclero-therapy needle was passed through the endoscope and positioned at the level of the esophageal stricture. With careful manipulation of the needle tip, the endoscope injected steroid solution into the strictured segment in a four-quadrant method.

    The appropriate CPT codes for this case are
    A. 43456, 43201
    B. 43201, 43220
    C. 43249, 43236
    D. 43204, 43236

37. A 4-year-old patient presents for a bilateral adenoidectomy; bilateral myringotomy, and nasal antral windows under general anesthesia. The appropriate coding for this service is

    A. 42830, 3 1020-50, 69421-50
    B. 42830-50, 31020-50, 69436-50
    C. 42835, 31020, 69421
    D. 42840, 31020, 69421

38. A surgeon fuses the C6 and T-2 vertebrae of a patient after performing an arthrodesis to prepare the interspace. The appropriate CPT coding for this procedure is

A. 22556, 22585, 22585-59
B. 22554-51, 22585
C. 22556
D. 22585, 22585-59

39. Gertrude, a 55-year-old with painful fibroids, menorrhagia, a urethro-cele, and a recto-cele, agreed to surgery. Her gynecologist performed a vaginal hysterectomy and a combined anteroposterior colporrhaphy. What code(s) should be reported for this service?

    A. 58262
    B. 58262, 57260
    C. 58262, 57260-51
    D. 58262, 57260-59

40. Code for a coronary artery bypass with two coronary arterial grafts.

    A. 33533 x 2
    B. 33533, 33534
    C. 33534
    D. 33535

41. Code for a deep excision of a 0.8-cm lipoma underneath the scalp, followed by a layered closure of the 2.0-cm incision.

    A. 11421, 12031
    B. 11421, 12032
    C. 11422, 12031
    D. 11423, 12031

42. A Medicare patient underwent a ureteroscopic fulguration of a lesion with cystoscopic replacement of a ureteral stent. The correct CPT code(s) for reporting this service would be

    A. 52338, 52310-59.
    B. 52332, 52310
    C. 52338, 52310-59, 52332
    D. 52310, 52283-59

43. A procedure that is coded 19160-50 indicates that

    A. partial mastectomies were performed on both breasts during one operative session
    B. partial mastectomies were performed on both breasts during separate operative sessions
    C. a partial mastectomy was performed on one breast, and then later, during another operative session, the rest of the breast was removed
    D. a radical mastectomy was performed on both breasts during one operative session

44. A surgeon makes an incision to expose a prolapsing fat pad in the right lower eyelid, opens the septum at the junction with the rim, and dissects the fat pads. The fat pad nearest the canthus was resected and then the tear duct was repaired by tucking prolapsing fat from the nasal and central pat pads.
    The most accurate coding for this procedure would be

A. 15820
B. 15820, 12031
C. 15821, 12031
D. 15821

45. A surgeon removes a dacryolith from the nasolacrimal canal. The appropriate CPT and diagnostic codes are

    A. 68530, 375.55
    B. 68530, 375.57
    C. 68540, 375.55
    D. 68540, 375.4

46. A surgeon performs a tubal ligation on both the right and left Fallopian tubes. The procedure should be coded

    A. 58600-50
    B. 58600-LT, 58600-RT
    C. 58600, 58601
    D. 58600

Miscellaneous

47. Code for amphotericin B liposome, injection, 10 mg.

    A. C9121
    B. J0288
    C. J0289
    D. J0592

48. A fracture in which the bone splits longitudinally-especially in children-is known as a _____ fracture.

    A. impacted
    B. hairline
    C. greenstick
    D. comminuted

49. Anesthesia codes are located in the Anesthesia section as well as the _____ section of the CPT Manual.

    A. Evaluation & Management
    B. Category II
    C. Surgery
    D. Medicine

50. A patient reports to the emergency room complaining of lower back pain that has persisted for nearly a month. The radiologist performs a lum-bosacral spine x-ray, complete with oblique views. The appropriate CPT and diagnostic codes for this visit are

    A. 72100, 724.0
    B. 72100, 724.2
    C. 72110, 724.02
    D. 72114, 724.2

50._____

KEY (CORRECT ANSWERS)

1. D	11. D	21. B	31. A	41. A
2. B	12. A	22. C	32. B	42. A
3. B	13. B	23. B	33. A	43. A
4. C	14. C	24. A	34. C	44. D
5. B	15. A	25. C	35. B	45. B
6. C	16. B	26. C	36. B	46. D
7. B	17. A	27. A	37. A	47. C
8. B	18. C	28. A	38. A	48. C
9. C	19. D	29. B	39. C	49. D
10. A	20. B	30. B	40. C	50. B

EXAMINATION SECTION
TEST 1

DIRECTIONS: Each question or incomplete statement is followed by several suggested answers or completions. Select the one that BEST answers the question or completes the statement. *PRINT THE LETTER OF THE CORRECT ANSWER IN THE SPACE AT THE RIGHT.*

Medical Terminology

1. The term "papilloma" denotes a tumor that appears 1.____

   A. on a gland
   B. darkly pigmented
   C. as a small elevation
   D. in a scaly form

2. What is the term used to describe blood that is detectable by chemical test in stool or urine specimens? 2.____

   A. Meconium
   B. Precipitate
   C. Occult
   D. Residual

3. The mediastinum is 3.____

   A. the collapse of a lung with escape of air into the cavity between the lung and the chest wall
   B. the space in the middle of the chest between the lungs
   C. a malignant tumor occurring in the pleura, peritoneum or pericardium
   D. the membranous lining of the upper body cavity and covering for the lungs

4. Which of the following medical terms is used to denote a calculus in the pancreas? 4.____

   A. pancreatorrhaphy
   B. pancreatolith
   C. pancreatotomy
   D. pancreatopathy

5. Deficits in phosphorus and calcium sometimes cause a softening of the bone tissue, known as 5.____

   A. dysorthosis
   B. osteomalacia
   C. chondrostasis
   D. osteoporosis

6. In medical terms, which of the following is a suffix that means "pain"? 6.____

   A. -algia
   B. -osis
   C. -itis
   D. -taxia

7. The medical term describing an abnormally low amount of urine is

   A. polyuria
   B. oliguria
   C. uripenia
   D. anuria

8. In medical terms, the word "cephalocaudal" is a directional adjective describing a view or line that is directed

   A. side to middle
   B. front to back
   C. back and above
   D. head to tail

9. The medical term describing unequal pupil size is

   A. anisocoria
   B. strabismus
   C. corectasia
   D. ptosis

ICD-9-CM

10. Which of the following V codes should NEVER be used as a principal diagnosis?

    A. V24
    B. V29
    C. V62
    D. V58.5

11. An elderly woman is admitted to the emergency room after slipping on ice on her front porch and falling down several stairs. She landing hard on her right hip, and the fall resulted in right femoral neck fracture. What diagnosis codes should be reported?

    A. 820.9, E882.
    B. 821.3, E8880
    C. 820.8, E880.9
    D. 821.00

12. A child is brought to the emergency room in a coma after ingesting his mother's Thorazine. The correct diagnostic code for this case is

    A. 780.01, 969.1, E980.3
    B. 969.1, E980.3, 780.01
    C. 969.1, E853.0, 780.01
    D. 780.01, 969.1, E853.0

13. A patient suffered an acute CVA with infarction with left-sided hemiplegia, aphasia, and dysphagia. The hemiplegia and dysphagia cleared before discharge; only aphasia was present at discharge to rehabilitation. The appropriate diagnostic coding is

A. 434.91, 784.3
B. 434.91, 342.90, 787.2
C. 434.91, 342.90
D. 434.91, 342.90, 784.3, 787.2

14. Code for Alzheimer's dementia with behavioral disturbance:

    A. 331.0
    B. 331.0, 294.10
    C. 331.0, 294.11
    D. 331.2, 294.10

15. A patient's systolic blood pressure is over 160, but the patient has no history of hypertension, and the physician is reluctant to make this diagnosis based on a single visit. The diagnostic code for this visit would be

    A. 401.1
    B. 401.9
    C. 642.30
    D. 796.2

16. A patient is admitted with multiple burns. The FIRST code listed should be the one that reflects the

    A. highest degree of burn
    B. greatest single surface area of the body that has been burned
    C. exact number of burns
    D. least serious burn

17. Chapter 11 codes should be used unless pregnancy is incidental to the encounter, in which instance code _____ should be used in place of any Chapter 11 codes.

    A. 650
    B. V22.0
    C. V22.2
    D. E849.9

Payment Methodologies

18. A provider who accepts "assignment" for a Medicare patient

    A. is required to charge half or less of his/her customary fee
    B. is required to collect the patient's copayment up front
    C. agrees to collect the payment directly from the patient
    D. agrees to have Medicare pay him/her directly

19. A physician who expects a patient to remain in the hospital for more than 24 hours should

    A. keep the patient in observation for eight hours and admit the patient after that time period
    B. admit the patient for the time limit of observation
    C. admit the patient as an inpatient
    D. admit the patient to observation

20. Which of the following would be NOT included in the facility fee charge? 20.____

    A. Ambulance services
    B. Nursing services
    C. Housekeeping services
    D. Anesthesia materials

21. On CMS 1500, the number in box 24e should correspond to the one diagnosis code in box 21 that supports the procedure. This refers to 21.____

    A. revenue codes
    B. a crossover claim
    C. an EOB
    D. the linkage of ICD-9-CM and CPT codes

22. What is a "grouper?" 22.____

    A. Software that translates variables into DRGs
    B. Software used by Medicare hospitals to process outpatient claims
    C. A measure of the difference in resources among physician fee schedule areas
    D. Software that tracks the flow of a claim through the hospital and the different departments.

23. FL 16 of CMS 1450 is coded "X." This means that the patient 23.____

    A. is legally separated
    B. is divorced
    C. has no dependents
    D. died in the hospital

24. A procedure code with the status modifier _____ denotes a procedure that is NOT paid under Medicare OPPS. 24.____

    A. E   B. G   C. K   D. X

25. If a patient is injured while at work, one of the form locators (FLs) from 24-30 on CMS 1450 should be coded 25.____

    A. 01   B. 02   C. 03   D. 05

General CPT

26. The "surgical package" for major surgery contains a minimum _____ day postoperative period that includes all visits to the physician during that time unless the visit is for a totally different reason than that for the surgery. 26.____

    A. 30   B. 60   C. 90   D. 120

27. Code an extended second-opinion consult required by an HMO.   27._____

   A. 99271
   B. 99205-99
   C. 99274-32
   D. 99275-23

28. Modifier 76 is used to indicate a(n)   28._____

   A. unrelated procedure or service by the same physician during the postoperative period of the original surgery
   B. repeat procedure on the same day by another physician
   C. return trip to the operating room for a related procedure during the postoperative period of the original surgery
   D. repeat procedure on the same day by the same physician

29. 36 days after a patient had a lesion removed from her breast, the entire breast was removed in a modified radical mastectomy that included the axillary lymph nodes and the pectoralis minor muscle, but excluded the pectoralis major muscle. The correct code for this second procedure would be   29._____

   A. 19120, 19240
   B. 19220-58
   C. 19240-58
   D. 19240

30. Code a limited study for transthoracic echocardiogram for congenital cardiac anomalies.   30._____

   A. 93304x2
   B. 93304-26
   C. 93303
   D. 93304

31. In the CPT manual, a coder comes across an entry that is preceded by the symbol _. This means that   31._____

   A. conscious sedation is included in the procedure
   B. is linked to a CPT Assistant article
   C. the code is exempt from the use of modifier 51
   D. it is a Level III code

32. A plus sign (+) that appears before a code in the CPT manual indicates that the code   32._____

   A. is an add-on code that cannot be used alone
   B. indicates a new procedure that has been added since the most recent edition of the CPT manual
   C. involves special instructions
   D. is modifier 51 exempt

33. "Information Only" modifiers–which do not impact reimbursement–include each of the following, EXCEPT   33._____

   A. 22   B. 24   C. 32   D. 57

34. Code for a laparoscopic fimbrioplasty.

    A. 58672
    B. 58673
    C. 58750
    D. 58760

35. A patient with attention deficit/hyperactivity disorder (ADDH) visits an outpatient hospital and receives 25 minutes of individual psychotherapy that was insight-oriented and aimed at modifying behavior. The most appropriate code for this visit is

    A. 90816, 314.1
    B. 90806, 314.01
    C. 90804, 314.00
    D. 90804, 314.01

Surgical Procedures

36. Code for the amputation of the left leg through the tibia and fibula.

    A. 27759
    B. 27880
    C. 27881
    D. 27882

37. A 74-year-old woman with gastric cancer and a subcutaneous port presents with a poorly functioning port. Infusion and injections can be made, but blood cannot be aspirated. A vascular snare is placed in the vein through the catheter, and the tip of the central venous catheter is engaged with the snare. The fibrin sheath and thrombus are stripped from the catheter.

    The appropriate CPT code for the procedure is

    A. 36861
    B. 36536
    C. 35476
    D. 36870

38. A patient reports to the emergency room with a torn fingernail and a subungual hematoma on his nail bed. After the patient's right hand was soaked in Hibiclens for more than five minutes, a digital block was performed with 1:1 solution of Marcaine 0.5% and Lidocaine 2%. Under sterile technique the nail was removed, revealing a transverse V-shaped nail bed laceration. No crepitus was noted. The laceration was irrigated with saline and Hibiclens solution, and the nail bed laceration was repaired with #5-0 Vicryl x 3. The nail plate was reattached in the eponychial fold and secured with three #4-0 nylon sutures. The wound was cleaned and a bulky dressing was applied.
    The correct CPT code(s) to report this service would be:

    A. 11760
    B. 11730, 11760
    C. 01999, 11730, 11760
    D. 01999, 11760, 11730-51

39. Using an ophthalmic endoscope, a physician exchanges a patient's intraocular lenses. The appropriate code for this procedure is

    A. 66986, 66990
    B. 66985, 66990
    C. 66986
    D. 66985

40. A surgeon, while excising a suspicious pigmented lesion on a patient's calf, makes an incision of about 5 cm. The lesion is found to measure more than 5 cm, and retraction of the skin edges does not allow primary closure. After extensive skin undermining, the wound repair was completed. The most appropriate coding for this procedure would be

    A. 11606, 13121
    B. 11606
    C. 11606, 12032
    D. 11600, 13121

41. A patient is prepared for surgery to repair a spigelian hernia. Before anesthesia is administered, the physician decides the procedure should not be performed. This should

    A. not be coded
    B. be coded as 49590, with a an attached explanatory note
    C. 49590-52
    D. 49590-73

42. A patient reports to emergency room after a fall. The ER physician performs a layered closure of a 3 cm laceration of the patient's upper arm, and a simple suture of a .5 cm laceration of the patient's calf. The most appropriate coding for these procedures would be

    A. 99281, 12301, 12001
    B. 99281-25, 12302, 12001-59
    C. 12302, 12001-58
    D. 12302, 12001-59

43. A physician performed a preoperative placement of a needle localization wire in a patient's breast under radiological supervision. The code for this procedure is

    A. 19290
    B. 19290, 19291
    C. 19290, 76096
    D. 19290 x 2

44. The modifier LC, attached to a surgical code, means that the procedure

    A. was performed on the left coronary artery
    B. was performed on the left side
    C. is an ambulatory surgical center service
    D. is expected to be denied as not reasonable and necessary

45. Prior to performing a tympanostomy in both ears, a physician removed the impacted cerumen in the right ear in order to enable surgery. The most appropriate CPT coding for these procedures is

    A. 69210-R, 69433
    B. 69433-50, 69210-59
    C. 69433-50
    D. 69210-59, 69433-50

46. Code for a right modified radical mastectomy, including the axillary lymph nodes, without any muscles.

    A. 19160
    B. 19200
    C. 19220
    D. 19240

Miscellaneous

47. A 70-year-old patient, who has breast cancer herself and a family history of colon cancer, undergoes a screening colonoscopy in her physician's office. The most appropriate code for this procedure is

    A. G0121-53
    B. G0105, 45378
    C. G0105
    D. G0121

48. The modifier GN, attached to a surgical code, indicates a(n)

    A. screening mammogram and diagnostic mammogram on the same patient on the same day
    B. service delivered under an outpatient occupational therapy plan of care
    C. item or service statutorily excluded from Medicare coverage
    D. service delivered under an outpatient speech language pathology plan of care

49. Code for 48 hours of prolonged extracorporeal circulation for cardiopulmonary insufficiency.

    A. 33960
    B. 33960 x2
    C. 33961 x 2
    D. 33960;33961

50. What is the term for a diagnostic test that uses a specific antibody or antigen to detect the presence of an analyte?

    A. Immunoassay
    B. Assay
    C. Panel
    D. Series

KEY (CORRECT ANSWERS)

1. C	11. C	21. D	31. C	41. D
2. C	12. C	22. A	32. B	42. B
3. B	13. A	23. A	33. A	43. C
4. B	14. C	24. A	34. A	44. A
5. B	15. D	25. B	35. D	45. C
6. A	16. A	26. C	36. B	46. D
7. B	17. C	27. C	37. B	47. C
8. D	18. D	28. D	38. A	48. D
9. A	19. A	29. C	39. A	49. D
10. C	20. A	30. B	40. A	50. A

TEST 2

DIRECTIONS: Each question or incomplete statement is followed by several suggested answers or completions. Select the one that BEST answers the question or completes the statement. *PRINT THE LETTER OF THE CORRECT ANSWER IN THE SPACE AT THE RIGHT.*

Medical Terminology

1. In medical terms, the suffix "-oid" means   1._____

   A. of or pertaining to
   B. straight
   C. around or near
   D. like or resembling

2. A cholecystectomy is an excision of the   2._____

   A. spleen
   B. gallbladder
   C. renal gland
   D. liver

3. In medical terminology, a diminutive suffix forms a word that designates a small version   3._____
   of an object indicated by the word root. Which of the following is NOT a diminutive suffix?

   A. -ole
   B. -ula
   C. -ina
   D. -icle

4. The pineal gland is a   4._____

   A. part of the brain located beneath teh cerebral hemispheres and next to the third
      ventricle, which serves as a relay station for nerve impulses in the brain.
   B. region of the brain located below the thalamus, forming the major portion of the
      ventral region of the diencephalon.
   C. small reddish-gray body that is part of the epithalamus
   D. pea-sized endocrine gland that sits in a small, bony cavity at the base of the brain

5. Myasthenia gravis is a condition of the   5._____

   A. muscles
   B. lymph
   C. nerves
   D. endocrine system

6. The medical term that describes an inflammation of the salivary gland is   6._____

   A. sialitis
   B. linguosis
   C. stomatitis
   D. gingivitis

7. The medical abbreviation AD is often used to designate the 7.____

   A. left eye
   B. right eye
   C. left ear
   D. right ear

8. The medical term that denotes a decrease or insufficiency of white blood cells is 8.____

   A. hypoleukocytis
   B. leukans
   C. leukocytopenia
   D. leukocytemia

9. Salpingitis is a word that refers to inflammation of the 9.____

   A. ovary
   B. uterus
   C. vagina
   D. Fallopian tube

ICD-9-CM

10. Code for gangrenous necrotizing fascitis. The culture grew staphylococci. 10.____

    A. 728.86, 041.10
    B. 728.9, 785.4, 041.10
    C. 738.4, 041.10
    D. 728.86, 785.4, 041.10

11. Code for a history of a cerebral artery occlusion with infarction with residuals of hemiple- 11.____
    gia and aphasia.

    A. 434.91, 342.90, 784.3
    B. 438.20
    C. 438.20, 438.11
    D. 784.3, 434.91

12. A woman reports for a scheduled mammogram. She has been flagged as a high-risk 12.____
    patient because her mother had breast cancer. The mammogram is conducted and
    reveals no abnormalities. What is the principal diagnosis code?

    A. V76.1   B. V76.11
    C. V76.12   D. 611.72

13. A patient reports to the emergency room with intense chest pains, shortness of breath, 13.____
    and a dry cough. The patient was recently diagnosed with gonorrhea. The physician
    diagnoses him with acute gonococcal pericarditis.
    The best code for this diagnosis is

    A. 420.90, 098.80   B. 098.83
    C. 420.0, 098.83   D. 420.99

14. A patient has systemic lupus erythematosus, which has caused her to suffer from chronic nephritis. What diagnosis codes should be reported?

    A. 710, 581.81
    B. 583.81, 710.0
    C. 582.81, 710.0
    D. 710.0, 582.81

15. For coding purposes, an excisional debridement of a burn wound that is NOT performed by a physician would be coded

    A. 86.22
    B. 86.28
    C. 85.69
    D. 93.57

16. A patient was standing on a stepladder on his patio, pruning bushes, when he falls onto the patio and sustains a brain stem injury. He loses consciousness and never regains consciousness, and dies within 48 hours. The most accurate code for this episode is

    A. 854.05, E881.0, E849.0
    B. 854.15, E884.2
    C. 854.04, E882.0, E849.7
    D. 854.05, E881.0

17. A burn victim has been admitted to the hospital very recently, and in her diagnosis the physician has not specified the site of the burn. The coder should assign a code from category

    A. 942
    B. 946
    C. 948
    D. 949

Payment Methodologies

18. Which of the following is a key characteristic of the Ambulatory Payment Classification (APC)?

    A. Payment for inpatient services
    B. Payment based on fee schedule
    C. Assignment determined through HCPCS system
    D. Fee-for-service payment

19. On CMS 1450, the patient control number is entered in field

    A. Ia
    B. 1
    C. 3
    D. 12

20. The purpose of pass-through payments is to

    A. supplement the cost for payment under the Ambulatory Payment Classification (APC)
    B. reduce the hospital charges for each item billed by using the hospital cost-to-charges ratio
    C. reduce standard payments amounts for an Ambulatory Payment Classification (APC)
    D. eliminate payments for drugs and biologicals

21. Which of the following would be a valid "place of service" code for field 24b of CMS 1500?

    A. 32
    B. 27
    C. 47
    D. 11

22. A patient's medical record number is entered in form locator (FL) _____ of CMS 1450.

    A. 1
    B. 5
    C. 23
    D. 35

23. Each of the following services is covered by Part B Medicare, EXCEPT

    A. home health care
    B. outpatient hospital care
    C. inpatient hospital care
    D. physician's services

24. Of the following, the best definition of "revenue center" is

    A. a system for reimbursing inpatient hospital costs
    B. a facility cost center for which a separate charge is billed on an institutional claim
    C. any facility, inpatient or outpatient, that participates in Medicare
    D. the standard for measuring the value of medical services provided by physicians

25. A procedure code with the status modifier _____ will result in payment for the item, drug or biological in addition to the APC reimbursement for the service performed.

    A. A
    B. B
    C. G
    D. X

General CPT

26. Which of the following is "10-day" CPT code?

    A. 12057
    B. 10060
    C. 15302
    D. 17108

27. Code for an anterior spinal fusion of L5-S1, with cages and bone grafting, for a spinal surgeon and a general surgeon working together. The general surgeon worked together on the anterior fusion, while assisting on the cages and grafts. The correct way to code for the general surgeon's participation in this operation would be:

    A. 22558-62
    B. 22558-62, 22851-62, 20937-62
    C. 22558-80, 22851-80, 20937-80
    D. 22558-62, 22851-80, 20937-80

28. The correct way to code for 90 minutes of critical care is

    A. 99291, 99175
    B. 99291, 99292
    C. 99295, 99292
    D. 99292, 99292, 99292

29. The code that should be used for arthroplasty of the toe is

    A. 28108
    B. 28124
    C. 28510
    D. 28899

30. Category II CPT codes are

    A. supplemental tracking codes that can be used for performance measurement, but not reimbursement
    B. alphanumeric codes intended to allow data tracking for emerging technology
    C. codes that are combined within the global surgical period
    D. new procedure codes that have been added since the most recent edition of the CPT manual

31. When a CPT code is "technical service only," it means that

    A. MOD-TC must always be added
    B. only the facility (hospital), would bill for services
    C. if the hospital wants to bill for professional services also, it should submit code MOD-26
    D. only the provider (physician) would bill for services

32. Code for the dilation of the esophagus with a 25-mm balloon.

    A. 43201
    B. 43220
    C. 43249
    D. 43456

33. Which of the following is a case management code?

    A. 99631
    B. 99490
    C. 99210
    D. 99815

34. For the initial evaluation of a problem for which a procedure is performed, modifier _____ is used.

    A. 24
    B. 25
    C. 32
    D. 51

35. Code for retrograde catheterization of the left heart from the femoral artery.

    A. 93501
    B. 93510
    C. 93511
    D. 93514

Surgical Procedures

36. A surgeon performed a bilateral levator resection for upper lid ptosis. The appropriate code is

    A. 67904 x 2
    B. 67904R, 67904L
    C. 67904-50
    D. 67904-51

37. Samantha, a 40-year-old with documented fibroids and anemia, scheduled surgery with her gynecologist. An ultrasound also identified a left ovarian cyst. Adriana underwent a supracervical hysterectomy, as had been discussed, but her Fallopian tubes and ovaries were left in place. At the same time, the gynecologist opened and drained the ovarian cyst and sent a biopsy of the cyst wall to pathology. She then removed the cyst capsule from Samantha's ovary. What code(s) should be reported for this service?

    A. 58180, 58925-51
    B. 58180, 58925-59
    C. 58180, 58925
    D. 58180

38. A patient underwent a stereotactic biopsy of her left breast. Following local anesthesia with approximately 5 cc of 1% Lidocaine, a small incision was made in the skin. An 11-gauge mammotome was inserted through the incision to the level of the microcalcifications following the stereotactic coordinates. Stereotactic images were obtained to confirm accurate positioning of the mammotome probe. The mechanical cutter was then activated, tissue was cut, excised and transported through the mammotome probe to the collection chamber. A Micromark sterile surgical clip was injected at the conclusion of the procedure to mark the biopsy site in the event of future surgical excision and to monitor future mammograms.
The correct CPT code(s) for reporting this service would be

    A. 19103, 19295-59
    B. J0704, 19103-LT, 19295-LT
    C. 19103-LT, 19295-LT
    D. 19103

39. A surgeon removes two malignant lesions—one measuring 3.0 cm, the other 1.8 cm—from a patient's hand, and follows each excision with a simple closure. The most appropriate way to code for this procedure is

    A. 11623 x 2, 12301 x 2
    B. 11623, 16223-59, 12301 x 2
    C. 11623, 16222
    D. There is not enough information to code for this procedure.

40. A surgeon performs an anterior cervical decompression and fusion while using an operating microscope with placement of Atlantis plating and a fibular strut allograft. The correct code for this procedure is

    A. 22554, 63075-51, 22845, 20931
    B. 22554, 63075-51, 22845, 69990, 20931
    C. 22554, 63075, 22845, 69990, 20931
    D. 22554, 63075, 22845

41. Extensive enterolysis of adhesions is performed during an inguinal hernial repair performed on a 55 year-old male using a mesh prosthesis. The appropriate code(s) to report this service is/are:

    A. 49505-22
    B. 49650-22
    C. 49505, 44005-59
    D. 49505, 49568, 44005-59

42. A patient with a congenital cleft lip had it repaired with closure of the alveolar ridge, which included a bone graft to the alveolar ridge. In addition, the nose was repaired, which involved a columellar lengthening of the septum that required a bone graft. Code for these procedures.

    A. 30462, 42210-50, 21210-50
    B. 30462, 42210-51, 21210-51
    C. 30420, 42210, 21210
    D. 30462, 42210, 21210

43. Code for arthrotomy of the wrist joint with biopsy and synovectomy.   43._____

    A. 25100, 25105-51
    B. 25105
    C. 25101
    D. 25100, 25105

44. During an office visit, a physician removes 24 small skin tags from a patient's back and neck. The most appropriate procedural code for this is   44._____

    A. 11200-51
    B. 11200
    C. 11200, 11201
    D. 11200, 11201-51

45. After performing a cystourethroscopy, a surgeon places an indwelling ureteral stent. Later that evening, the patient returns to the operating room to have the stent removed by the same surgeon. The modifier that should be used with the code for the removal is   45._____

    A. 51
    B. 58
    C. 76
    D. 78

46. Using two separate incisions, a hand surgeon removes two separate benign lesions, each measuring about 1.0 cm, from a patient's left hand. The appropriate procedure code would be   46._____

    A. 11401 x 2
    B. 11401
    C. 11400, 11401
    D. 11401, 11401-59

Miscellaneous

47. A ligation is a procedure that involves   47._____

    A. forcing a fluid into a vessel or cavity
    B. binding or tying off
    C. uniting parts by stitching them together
    D. suturing

48. The conjunctivo-Tarso Muller resection is a procedure that   48._____

    A. corrects for strabismus
    B. straightens a clubfoot
    C. repairs a ptotic upper eyelid
    D. minimizes scar tissue after grafts

49. Which of the following is an add-on code?   49.____

   A. 15201
   B. 28900
   C. 01951
   D. 42999

50. Curettage is a mode of treatment that involves   50.____

   A. puncturing an organ or tissue
   B. the removal of part or all of an organ
   C. removing a small piece of living tissue
   D. scraping away body tissue

KEY (CORRECT ANSWERS)

1. D	11. C	21. D	31. B	41. B
2. B	12. B	22. C	32. B	42. B
3. C	13. B	23. C	33. A	43. B
4. C	14. D	24. B	34. B	44. C
5. A	15. B	25. C	35. B	45. B
6. A	16. A	26. B	36. B	46. A
7. D	17. C	27. D	37. B	47. B
8. C	18. C	28. B	38. C	48. C
9. D	19. C	29. D	39. C	49. A
10. D	20. B	30. A	40. A	50. D

EXAMINATION SECTION
TEST 1

DIRECTIONS: Each question or incomplete statement is followed by several suggested answers or completions. Select the one that BEST answers the question or completes the statement. *PRINT THE LETTER OF THE CORRECT ANSWER IN THE SPACE AT THE RIGHT.*

QUESTIONS 1-25.

Questions 1-25 contain often used medical terms. Choose the lettered choice that is CLOSEST in meaning to the numbered items.

1. BIOPSY:

    A. routine physical
    B. exploratory surgery
    C. examination of living tissues
    D. excision of a tumor

2. CARDIOVASCULAR: relating to

    A. heart and blood vessels
    B. stress tests
    C. circulation in one's extremities
    D. blood supply to the muscles

3. CHOLECYSTECTOMY: excision of the

    A. kidneys   B. gall bladder
    C. pancreas   D. spleen

4. COAGULATION:

    A. thickening   B. dispersion
    C. separation into categories D. suffocation

5. CONGENITAL:

    A. relating to the reproductive organs
    B. sexually reproductive
    C. normal
    D. from birth

6. DORSAL: relating to

    A. the sides   B. aquatic animals
    C. the back   D. sharks only

7. EDEMA:

    A. cleansing of the digestive tract
    B. fluid in the joints
    C. a skin condition
    D. a food-borne disease

8. EMBOLISM:

   A. shortage of breath
   B. reddening of the skin
   C. deficiency of vitamin E
   D. sudden blockage of a vessel

8.____

9. FETUS:

   A. relating to foot disease
   B. physiological reaction to hunger
   C. unborn offspring
   D. infant

9.____

10. HEMATURIA:

    A. subdural blood clot
    B. red blood cell count
    C. blood cells in the urine
    D. platelet count

10.____

11. HEPATIC: relating to the

    A. liver   B. blood
    C. skin   D. leg muscles

11.____

12. INCIPIENT:

    A. in the final stages
    B. beginning to become apparent
    C. fatal
    D. intermediary

12.____

13. INFRACOSTAL:

    A. behind the lungs   B. near the spine
    C. above the ribs   D. below the ribs

13.____

14. LAPAROTOMY: surgical section of the

    A. lung   B. liver
    C. abdominal wall   D. heart

14.____

15. NECROSIS:

    A. obsession with corpses
    B. localized death of living tissue
    C. kidney disease
    D. state of deep depression

15.____

16. NEONATAL: relating to

    A. period before birth   B. gestation
    C. infancy   D. childhood

16.____

17. POSTPARTUM:

    A. after birth
    B. after death
    C. isolated during childhood
    D. quarantined

17._____

18. RENAL: relating to the

    A. kidneys
    B. colon
    C. adrenal gland
    D. throat

18._____

19. SARCOID: disease characterized by

    A. a sore throat
    B. a red, itchy rash
    C. growths on the heart
    D. nodules under the skin

19._____

20. SEPTIC: relating to

    A. poison
    B. sewage
    C. infection
    D. contamination

20._____

21. SEQUELA:

    A. aftereffect of a disease
    B. follow-up examination
    C. repeat of a surgical procedure
    D. medication after surgery

21._____

22. TACHYCARDIA:

    A. irregular pulse
    B. infection of the heart
    C. heart attack
    D. rapid heartbeat

22._____

23. TOXEMIA: a condition associated with

    A. lack of nutrients
    B. toxins in the blood
    C. loss of appetite
    D. ingestion of human wastes

23._____

24. TRAUMATIC:

    A. fatal
    B. contagions
    C. causing injury to tissue
    D. chronic

24._____

25. VENTRAL: relating to the

    A. respiratory system
    B. circulatory system
    C. belly
    D. palms of the hands

25._____

QUESTIONS 26-35.

In questions 26-35, choose the word that is spelled INCORRECTLY.

26. A. angioma B. cereberum 26.____
    C. dorsal D. embolism

27. A. urethra B. peritoneum 27.____
    C. deficiency D. duodinum

28. A. deltoid B. cardiac 28.____
    C. histerectomy D. colon

29. A. syringe B. ovarian 29.____
    C. vitamin D. legament

30. A. mussle B. transfusion 30.____
    C. rickets D. ulna

31. A. tendon B. subcutaneous 31.____
    C. ocipital D. fracture

32. A. metacarpal B. podiatry 32.____
    C. patela D. sprain

33. A. clavicle B. fallopian 33.____
    C. calcium D. pancreis

34. A. hematocrit B. surgicle 34.____
    C. tumor D. paroxysm

35. A. vertebri B. uterus 35.____
    C. hemoglobin D. toxicity

QUESTIONS 36-55.

Questions 36-55 refer to the lists below. List I contains the names of 20 diseases or conditions. List II gives the 17 major subdivisions of the International Statistical Classification of Diseases, Injuries, and Causes of Death. For each of the diseases or conditions given in List I, write in the space provided at the right for the corresponding number, the letter preceding the major subdivision into which the disease or condition properly falls. (The same letter may be used more than once.)

EXAMPLE: x. acute appendicitis. Since this is a disease of the digestive system, the answer should be "i."

LIST I		LIST II	
36.	abscess of scalp	A.	infective and parasitic diseases
37.	acute poliomyelitis	B.	neoplasms
38.	adhesive peritonitis	C.	allergic, endocrine system, metabolic and nutritional diseases
39.	aortic stenosis	D.	diseases of the blood and blood-forming organs
40.	arteriosclerosis	E.	mental, psychoneurotic and personality disorders
41.	burns and trauma due to explosion of stove	F.	diseases of the nervous system and sense organs
42.	cerebral hemorrhage	G.	diseases of the circulatory system
43.	chronic glomerular nephritis	H.	diseases of the respiratory system
44.	hypothyroidism	I.	diseases of the digestive system
45.	influenza	J.	diseases of the genitourinary system
46.	muscular dystrophy	K.	deliveries and complications of pregnancy, childbirth and the puerperium
47.	multiple sclerosis	L.	diseases of the skin and cellular tissue
48.	osteomyelitis	M.	diseases of the bones and organs of movement
49.	pernicious anemia	N.	congenital malformations
50.	postnatal asphyxia	O.	certain diseases of early infancy
51.	prolapse of umbilical cord	P.	symptoms, senility and ill-defined conditions
52.	pulmonary congestion	Q.	accidents, poisonings and violence
53.	rectal cancer		
54.	syphilis		
55.	ulcerative colitis		

36.____
37.____
38.____
39.____
40.____
41.____
42.____
43.____
44.____
45.____
46.____
47.____
48.____
49.____
50.____
51.____
52.____
53.____
54.____
55.____

KEY (CORRECT ANSWERS)

1.	C	16.	C	31.	C	46.	N
2.	A	17.	A	32.	C	47.	F
3.	B	18.	A	33.	D	48.	M
4.	A	19.	D	34.	B	49.	D
5.	D	20.	C	35.	A	50.	O
6.	C	21.	A	36.	L	51.	K
7.	B	22.	D	37.	F	52.	H
8.	D	23.	B	38.	L	53.	I
9.	C	24.	C	39.	G	54.	J
10.	C	25.	C	40.	G	55.	I
11.	A	26.	B	41.	G		
12.	B	27.	D	42.	F		
13.	D	28.	C	43.	J		
14.	C	29.	D	44.	C		
15.	B	30.	A	45.	A		

TEST 2

DIRECTIONS: Each question or incomplete statement is followed by several suggested answers or completions. Select the one that BEST answers the question or completes the statement. *PRINT THE LETTER OF THE CORRECT ANSWER IN THE SPACE AT THE RIGHT.*

QUESTIONS 1-5.

Questions 1-5 are to be answered *solely* on the basis of the following paragraphs.

"No person shall disinter a coffin or casket containing human remains unless a disinterment permit has been issued by the Department of Health, except when the disinterment is ordered by the Office of the Chief Medical Examiner. Application for a disinterment permit shall be submitted at the office of the Department of Health in the borough in which the remains are buried. The application shall be accompanied by an affidavit from the next of kin or other authorized person."

No person shall remove human remains from the place of death unless a removal permit has been issued by the Department of Health or authorization to remove has been granted by telephone. A removal permit or telephone authorization to remove does not authorize burial or cremation. Human remains shall not be brought into the City unless a permit for their transportation or burial has been issued by the authorized agency of the municipality or -county within the United States within whose jurisdiction death occurred. A burial permit issued by such agency which specifies the cemetery in which burial is to take place shall be accepted for burial in New York City. If, however, such permit specifies no cemetery or a cemetery other than the one intended for burial then application for a permit must be made to the Department of Health. No permit to cremate shall be issued unless the application is accompanied by an affidavit from the next of kin or other authorized person, and unless the application is approved by the Office of the Chief Medical Examiner.

On the basis of the information given above, determine which of the following statements are TRUE and which are FALSE. Indicate your answer by using (T) for TRUE and (F) for FALSE.

1. A body now buried in Brooklyn is to be reburied in Queens. A permit to disinter must be obtained from the Queens office of the Department of Health.   1.____

2. The Office of the Chief Medical Examiner must approve an application to disinter a body.   2.____

3. A person who has died in Manhattan is to be buried in Staten Island. The Department of Health may give permission by telephone to have the body taken to Staten Island and buried there.   3.____

4. A permit is sought to cremate a dead body. Even though the Office of the Chief Medical Examiner agrees to the cremation, the next of kin or other authorized person must submit an affidavit.   4.____

5. A woman calls and tells the medical clerk that her cousin just died in Columbus, Ohio. She wants the body buried in Brooklyn, New York. The medical clerk should tell her that a burial permit must be obtained from the Brooklyn office of the Department of Health.   5.____

QUESTIONS 6-12.

Questions 6-12 refer to the following code tables which are to be used for classifying cases of death.

TABLE I			TABLE II			TABLE III	
Code	Sex	Code	Age		Code	Cause of Death	
X	Male	01	Under 1 year		10	Heart Disease	
Y	Female	02	1-10 years		20	Poliomyelitis	
		03	11-20 years		30	Cancer	
		04	21-30 years		40	Meningitis	
		05	31-40 years		50	Accident	
		06	41-50 years		60	Other	
		07	51-60 years				
		08	Over 60 years				

TABLE IV			TABLE V		TABLE VI	
	Borough Where		Present			Marital
Code	Person Died	Code	Occupation	Code		Status
1	Manhattan	101	Professional	a		Single
2	Brooklyn	102	Office Worker	b		Married
3	Bronx	103	Skilled Worker	c		Divorced
4	Queens	104	Unskilled Worker	d		Widowed
5	Richmond	105	Housewife			
		106	Student			
		107	Other			

Below are 7 cases of death which are to be classified. In accordance with the code tables given above, assign the proper code number to each case. The codes are to be arranged from left to right, in the order indicated by the numbers of the six code tables. <u>EXAMPLE</u>: A 3-year-old girl died in Richmond of meningitis. Her code number is: Y-02-40-5-107-a.

6. A 12-year-old high school boy died in the Bronx of injuries sustained in a traffic collision. 6.____

7. A 53-year-old clerk, divorced, died of a heart attack while shoveling snow in front of his home in Queens. 7.____

8. A 70-year-old widow, a housewife, died of cancer in a Queens hospital after a short stay. 8.____

9. A 37-year-old married porter died of pneumonia in his home in Brooklyn. 9.____

10. A 24-year-old lawyer, divorced from her husband, died in Manhattan of poliomyelitis. 10.____

11. A 4-month-old infant girl died in a Richmond hospital of a malformed kidney. 11.____

12. A 47-year-old machinist, married, died in the Bronx of injuries resulting from a fall at his place of employment. 12.____

QUESTIONS 13-22.

Questions 13-22 are to be answered based on the rules of filing. Column I containing the numbers 13-22, lists the names of 10 death certificates which are to be filed. Column II contains the heading of file drawers into which you are to file the certificates. For each number 13-22, choose the correct lettered file drawer and indicate said letter in the space at the right.

EXAMPLE: Eileen Sacks. The certificate of Eileen Sacks shouldbe filed in drawer headed Sa - Scl. The answer, therefore, would be A.

Column I

13. Donald Spiller
14. Stuart Simon
15. Sidney Schofield
16. Mark Stetner
17. Nelson Sklar
18. Daisy Saunders
19. Peter Sharpman
20. Arnold Snyder
21. Nathan Sentner
22. Marion Stoup

Column II

A. Drawer 1. Sa - Scl
B. Drawer 2. Sco - Ses
C. Drawer 3. Set - Sik
D. Drawer 4. Sil - Sni
E. Drawer 5. Sno - Suc

13.____
14.____
15.____
E. 16.____
17.____
18.____
19.____
20.____
21.____
22.____

QUESTIONS 23-30.

In questions 23-30, choose the letter that corresponds to the correct answer.

23. Assume that total deaths in one year amounted to 80,000. If heart disease accounted for 44% of these deaths, how many people died of all other causes?   23.____

   A. 35,200   B. 79,000   C. 44,800   D. 80,000

24. Assume that, of 885 people who died of hepatitis during a given year, 1/3 died between January 1 and May 31. What was the average number of deaths per month between January and May?   24.____

   A. 59   B. 295   C. 147   D. 49

25. Of 1200 deaths from diabetes in one year, 1/4 were in Manhattan and 1/6 in the Bronx. Of the remaining number, 2/5 were in Brooklyn. How many deaths from diabetes occurred in Brooklyn?   25.____

   A. 200   B. 300   C. 280   D. 500

26. Assume that in one year there were 840 deaths from all causes among a given age group. If 247 people died as a result of accidents and 73 died as a result of homicides, what percentage of people in this group died as a result of accidents and homicides (taken together)?

   A. 29   B. 38   C. 73   D. 84

27. Assume that in 2000, deaths from tuberculosis were 1400 and deaths from diabetes were 1260. If in 2001 deaths from tuberculosis declined to 1120, and deaths from diabetes declined at the same rate, how many deaths from diabetes occurred in 2001?

   A. 1008   B. 1120   C. 1260   D. 1400

28. In a given year, the number of deaths from enteritis, duodenitis and colitis totalled 280. The following year, deaths from enteritis remained the same and deaths from duodenitis increased; total deaths from the 3 causes was 250. Did deaths from colitis increase, decrease, or remain the same?

   A. Increased   B. Decreased
   C. Remained the same   D. Cannot be determined

29. Assume that 200 men and 100 women died of influenza in one year. If the next year the total number of such deaths remained the same, but 25% fewer died of influenza, how many women died of influenza?

   A. 100   B. 110   C. 125   D. 150

30. Assume that in one year, in the 45 to 64 year age group, 17,000 men and 10,000 women died. Of this number, 23% of the men and 35% of the women died of malignant neoplasms. In the 65 year and over age group, 25,000 men and 23,000 women died. Of this number, 19% of the men and 16% of the women died of malignant neoplasms.
    Of these 4 groups of people, which had the largest number of deaths from malignant neoplasms?

   A. Men, 45-64 years   B. Women, 45-64 years
   C. Men, 65 and over   D. Women, 65 and over

KEY (CORRECT ANSWERS)

1. F
2. F
3. T
4. T
5. F

6. X-03-50-3-106-a
7. X-07-10-4-102-c
8. Y-08-30-4-105-d
9. X-05-60-2-104-b
10. Y-04-20-1-101-c

11. Y-01-60-5-107-a
12. X-06-50-3-103-b
13. E
14. D
15. A

16. E
17. D
18. A
19. C
20. E

21. B
22. E
23. C
24. A
25. C

26. B
27. A
28. B
29. D
30. C

EXAMINATION SECTION
TEST 1

DIRECTIONS: Each question or incomplete statement is followed by several suggested answers or completions. Select the one that BEST answers the question or completes the statement. *PRINT THE LETTER OF THE CORRECT ANSWER IN THE SPACE AT THE RIGHT.*

Questions 1-15.

DIRECTIONS: In the following questions numbered 1 through 15, the word in capitals is the name of an anatomical part which is a segment of a larger structure or system For each question, select the letter preceding the structure or system of which the word in capitals is a part.

1. ESOPHAGUS

    A. circulatory system
    C. submaxillary
    B. bronchi
    D. respiratory system

2. ALVEOLI

    A. nervous system
    C. endocrine system
    B. lungs
    D. muscle

3. DELTOID

    A. upper arm
    C. circulatory system
    B. rib cage
    D. superior vena cava

4. FEMORAL ARTERY

    A. right ventricle
    C. circulatory system
    B. left auricle
    D. lymphatic system

5. BRACKIAL PLEXUS

    A. circulatory system
    C. respiratory system
    B. nervous system
    D. bronchi

6. ERYTHROCYTE

    A. lymph glands
    C. blood
    B. skeletal system
    D. large intestine

7. STERNUM

    A. spinal column
    C. nervous system
    B. muscular system
    D. skeletal system

8. THYMUS

    A. endocrine system
    C. parathyroids
    B. pituitary gland
    D. adrenals

9. MANDIBLE

    A. pelvis   B. head   C. liver   D. stomach

97

10. PECTORAL

    A. skeletal system   B. patella
    C. chest   D. digestive tract

11. CORNEA

    A. arm   B. eye   C. blood   D. lymph

12. CRANIUM

    A. circulatory system   B. left auricle
    C. skeletal system   D. abdomen

13. TRAPEZIUS

    A. breastbone   B. muscular system
    C. endocrine system   D. spinal column

14. MEGALOBLAST

    A. blood   B. pelvis   C. spleen   D. head

15. ADRENAL

    A. mouth   B. respiratory system
    C. liver   D. endocrine system

Questions 16-25.

DIRECTIONS: The following questions numbered 16 through 25 are concerned with various categories of diseases. For each question, select the letter preceding the disease or condition which MOST properly belongs to the category listed.

16. BONE DISEASE

    A. arrhythmia   B. arthritis
    C. edema   D. gastritis

17. DISEASE OF THE DIGESTIVE SYSTEM

    A. diabetes   B. osteomyelitis
    C. ileitis   D. conjunctivitis

18. DISEASE OF THE RESPIRATORY SYSTEM

    A. cyanosis   B. poliomyelitis
    C. jaundice   D. bronchiectasis

19. DISEASE OF THE HEART

    A. hepatitis   B. influenza
    C. encephalitis   D. myocarditis

20. DISEASE OF THE BLOOD

    A. leukemia   B. diphtheria
    C. pneumonia   D. colitis

21. NUTRITIONAL DISEASE 21.____

    A. hyperemia   B. mononucleosis
    C. trichinosis   D. scurvy

22. DISEASE OF THE NERVOUS SYSTEM 22.____

    A. amebiasis   B. parkinsonism
    C. ascariasis   D. tapeworm

23. PARASITIC DISEASE 23.____

    A. salmonella   B. neuralgia
    C. hemophilia   D. bursitis

24. SKIN DISEASE 24.____

    A. hydrocephalus   B. leprosy
    C. adenitis   D. angina

25. DISEASE OF THE URINARY TRACT 25.____

    A. myasthenia gravis   B. colitis
    C. hydronephrosis   D. dermatitis

KEY (CORRECT ANSWERS)

1.	D	11.	B
2.	B	12.	C
3.	A	13.	B
4.	C	14.	A
5.	B	15.	D
6.	C	16.	B
7.	D	17.	C
8.	A	18.	D
9.	B	19.	D
10.	C	20.	A

21. D
22. B
23. A
24. B
25. C

TEST 2

DIRECTIONS: Each question or incomplete statement is followed by several suggested answers or completions. Select the one that BEST answers the question or completes the statement. *PRINT THE LETTER OF THE CORRECT ANSWER IN THE SPACE AT THE RIGHT.*

Questions 1-10.

DIRECTIONS: Questions 1 through 10 are concerned with various categories of diseases. For each question, select the letter preceding the disease or condition which MOST properly belongs to the category listed.

1. DISEASE OF THE HEART 1.____
   - A. diabetes
   - B. tachycardia
   - C. osteoporosis
   - D. adenitis

2. SKIN DISEASE 2.____
   - A. cholelithiasis
   - B. colitis
   - C. psoriasis
   - D. encephalitis

3. DISEASE OF THE BLOOD 3.____
   - A. polycythemia
   - B. ileitis
   - C. psoitis
   - D. dermatitis

4. DISEASE OF THE RESPIRATORY SYSTEM 4.____
   - A. dysentery
   - B. angina
   - C. hemophilia
   - D. pneumonia

5. DISEASE OF THE DIGESTIVE SYSTEM 5.____
   - A. periastitis
   - B. bronchiectasis
   - C. enteritis
   - D. pertussis

6. PARASITIC DISEASE 6.____
   - A. ascariasis
   - B. nephritis
   - C. hyperemia
   - D. neuralgia

7. NUTRITIONAL DISEASE 7.____
   - A. entasis
   - B. pellagra
   - C. amebiasis
   - D. diphtheria

8. BONE DISEASE 8.____
   - A. gangrene
   - B. epilepsy
   - C. osteochondritis
   - D. bronchitis

9. DISEASE OF THE NERVOUS SYSTEM 9.____
   - A. mononucleosis
   - B. gallstones
   - C. jaundice
   - D. multiple sclerosis

10. DISEASE OF THE URINARY TRACT 10.____

    A. hydrocephalus   B. glomerulonephritis
    C. cyanosis   D. bursitis

Questions 11-25.

DIRECTIONS: For the following questions 11 through 25, select the letter preceding the part or system of the body which is CHIEFLY affected by the disease in capitals.

11. CONJUNCTIVITIS 11.____

    A. ear   B. intestines
    C. eye   D. liver

12. EMPHYSEMA 12.____

    A. heart   B. bronchial tubes
    C. pancreas   D. lymph nodes

13. CHOLELITHIASIS 13.____

    A. muscles   B. liver
    C. bones   D. common bile duct

14. PYELONEPHRITIS 14.____

    A. intestinal tract   B. arterial walls
    C. ligaments   D. urinary tract

15. EPILEPSY 15.____

    A. nervous system   B. pancreas
    C. thyroid   D. stomach

16. DYSENTERY 16.____

    A. tendons   B. kidneys
    C. intestines   D. brain

17. ERYTHROBLASTOSIS 17.____

    A. kidneys   B. blood
    C. endocrine system   D. large intestine

18. GLAUCOMA 18.____

    A. blood vessels   B. cortex
    C. cerebellum   D. eye

19. OSTEOPOROSIS 19.____

    A. bones   B. central nervous system
    C. adrenals   D. lymph nodes

20. MENINGITIS 20.____

    A. nasal passages   B. intestinal tract
    C. spinal cord   D. urinary tract

21. BURSITIS 21.____

    A. urinary tract   B. bones
    C. nasal passages   D. heart

22. ENDOCARDITIS 22.____

    A. cortex   B. kidneys   C. pancreas   D. heart

23. DIVERTICULOSIS 23.____

    A. thyroid   B. endocrine system
    C. intestinal tract   D. kidneys

24. ENCEPHALITIS 24.____

    A. brain   B. vessels   C. kidneys   D. eye

25. ILEITIS 25.____

    A. nervous system   B. blood
    C. liver   D. intestinal tract

KEY (CORRECT ANSWERS)

1.	B	11.	C
2.	C	12.	B
3.	A	13.	D
4.	D	14.	D
5.	C	15.	A
6.	A	16.	C
7.	B	17.	B
8.	C	18.	D
9.	D	19.	A
10.	B	20.	C

21. B
22. D
23. C
24. A
25. D

EXAMINATION SECTION
TEST 1

DIRECTIONS: Each question or incomplete statement is followed by several suggested answers or completions. Select the one that BEST answers the question or completes the statement. *PRINT THE LETTER OF THE CORRECT ANSWER IN THE SPACE AT THE RIGHT.*

Questions 1-20.

DIRECTIONS: Column I below lists words used in medical practice. Column II lists phrases which describe the words in Column I. Opposite the number preceding each of the words in Column I, place the letter preceding the phrase in Column II which BEST describes the word in Column I.

COLUMN I	COLUMN II
1. Abrasion	A. A disturbance of digestion
2. Aseptic	B. Destroying the germs of disease
3. Cardiac	C. A general poisoning of the blood
4. Catarrh	D. An instrument used for injecting fluids
5. Contamination	E. A scraping off of the skin
6. Dermatology	F. Free from disease germs
7. Disinfectant	G. An apparatus for viewing internal organs by means of x-rays
8. Dyspepsia	H. An instrument for assisting the eye in observing minute objects
9. Epidemic	I. An inoculable immunizing agent
10. Epidermis	J. The extensive prevalence in a community of a
11. Incubation	K. Chemical product of an organ
12. Microscope	L. Preceding birth
13. Pediatrics	M. Fever
14. Plasma	N. The branch of medical science that relates to the skin and its diseases
15. Prenatal	O. Fluid part of the blood
16. Retina	P. The science of the hygienic care of children
17. Syphilis	Q. Infection by contact
18. Syringe	R. Relating to the heart
19. Toxemia	S. Inner structure of the eye
20. Vaccine	T. Outer portion of the skin
	U. Pertaining to the ductless glands
	V. An infectious venereal disease
	W. The development of an infectious disease from the period of infection to that of the appearance of the first symptoms
	X. Simple inflammation of a mucous membrane
	Y. An instrument for measuring blood pressure

1.____
2.____
3.____
4.____
5.____
6.____
7.____
8.____
9.____
10.____
11.____
12.____
13.____
14.____
15.____
16.____
17.____
18.____
19.____
20.____

Questions 21-25.

DIRECTIONS: Each of Questions 21 through 25 consists of four words. Three of these words belong together. One word does NOT belong with the other three. For each group of words, you are to select the one word which does NOT belong with the other three words.

21. A. conclude   B. terminate   C. initiate   D. end   21.___

22. A. deficient   B. inadequate   22.___
    C. excessive   D. insufficient

23. A. rare   B. unique   C. unusual   D. frequent   23.___

24. A. unquestionable   B. uncertain   24.___
    C. doubtful   D. indefinite

25. A. stretch   B. contract   C. extend   D. expand   25.___

KEY (CORRECT ANSWERS)

1.	E	11.	W
2.	F	12.	H
3.	R	13.	P
4.	X	14.	O
5.	Q	15.	L
6.	N	16.	S
7.	B	17.	V
8.	A	18.	D
9.	J	19.	C
10.	T	20.	I

21. C
22. C
23. D
24. A
25. B

TEST 2

DIRECTIONS: Each question or incomplete statement is followed by several suggested answers or completions. Select the one that BEST answers the question or completes the statement. *PRINT THE LETTER OF THE CORRECT ANSWER IN THE SPACE AT THE RIGHT.*

Questions 1-4.

DIRECTIONS: Questions 1 through 4 pertain to the meaning of terms which may be encountered in laboratory work. For each question, select the option whose meaning is MOST NEARLY the same as that of the numbered item.

1. Atrophied

    A. enlarged B. relaxed
    C. strengthened D. wasted

    1.____

2. Leucocyte

    A. white cell B. red cell
    C. epithelial cell D. dermal cell

    2.____

3. Permeable

    A. volatile B. variable
    C. flexible D. penetrable

    3.____

4. Attenuate

    A. dilute B. infect
    C. oxidize D. strengthen

    4.____

Questions 5-11.

DIRECTIONS: For Questions 5 through 11, select the letter preceding the word which means MOST NEARLY the same as the first word.

5. legible

    A. readable B. eligible C. learned D. lawful

    5.____

6. observe

    A. assist B. watch C. correct D. oppose

    6.____

7. habitual

    A. punctual B. occasional
    C. usual D. actual

    7.____

8. chronological

    A. successive B. earlier
    C. later D. studious

    8.____

105

9. arrest
   A. punish   B. run   C. threaten   D. stop

10. abstain
    A. refrain   B. indulge   C. discolor   D. spoil

11. toxic
    A. poisonous   B. decaying
    C. taxing   D. defective

12. The *initial* contact is of great importance in setting a pattern for future relations.
    The word *initial*, as used in this sentence, means MOST NEARLY
    A. first   B. written   C. direct   D. hidden

13. The doctor prescribed a diet which was *adequate* for the patient's needs.
    The word *adequate*, as used in this sentence, means MOST NEARLY
    A. insufficient   B. unusual
    C. required   D. enough

14. The child was reported to be suffering from a vitamin *deficiency*.
    The word *deficiency*, as used in this sentence, means MOST NEARLY
    A. surplus   B. infection   C. shortage   D. injury

15. In obtaining medical case data, a medical record librarian should discourage the patient from giving *irrelevant* information.
    The word *irrelevant*, as used in this sentence, means MOST NEARLY
    A. too detailed   B. pertaining to relatives
    C. insufficient   D. inappropriate

16. The doctor requested that a *tentative* appointment be made for the patient.
    The word *tentative*, as used in this sentence, means MOST NEARLY
    A. definite   B. subject to change
    C. later   D. of short duration

17. The black plague resulted in an usually high *mortality rate* in the population of Europe.
    The term *mortality rate*, as used in this sentence, means MOST NEARLY
    A. future immunity of the people
    B. death rate
    C. general weakening of the health of the people
    D. sickness rate

18. The public health assistant was asked to file a number of *identical* reports on the case.
    The word *identical*, as used in this sentence, means MOST NEARLY
    A. accurate   B. detailed   C. same   D. different

19. The nurse assisted in *the biopsy* of the patient.
    The word *biopsy,* as used in this sentence, means MOST NEARLY

    A. autopsy
    B. excision and diagnostic study of tissue
    C. biography and health history
    D. administering of anesthesia

    19.____

20. The assistant noted that the swelling on the patient's face had *subsided.*
    The word *subsided,* as used in this sentence, means MOST NEARLY

    A. become aggravated   B. increased
    C. vanished   D. abated

    20.____

21. The patient was given food *intravenously.*
    The word *intravenously,* as used in this sentence, means MOST NEARLY

    A. orally   B. against his will
    C. through the veins   D. without condiment

    21.____

Questions 22-25.

DIRECTIONS: Each of Questions 22 through 25 consists of four words. Three of these words belong together. One word does NOT belong with the other three. For each group of words, you are to select the one word which does NOT belong with the other three words.

22.	A.	accelerate	B.	quicken	C.	accept	D.	hasten	22.____
23.	A.	sever	B.	rupture	C.	rectify	D.	tear	23.____
24.	A.	innocuous	B.	injurious	C.	dangerous	D.	harmful	24.____
25.	A.	adulterate			B.	contaminate			25.____
	C.	taint			D.	disinfect			

KEY (CORRECT ANSWERS)

1. D	11. A	21. C
2. A	12. A	22. C
3. D	13. D	23. C
4. A	14. C	24. A
5. A	15. D	25. D
6. B	16. B	
7. C	17. B	
8. A	18. C	
9. D	19. B	
10. A	20. D	

TEST 3

DIRECTIONS: Each question or incomplete statement is followed by several suggested answers or completions. Select the one that BEST answers the question or completes the statement. *PRINT THE LETTER OF THE CORRECT ANSWER IN THE SPACE AT THE RIGHT.*

Questions 1-25.

DIRECTIONS: Each of Questions 1 through 25 consists of a word, in capitals, followed by four suggested meanings of the word. For each question, indicate in the space at the right the letter preceding the word which means MOST NEARLY the same as the word in capitals.

1. TEMPORARY

    A. permanently
    B. for a limited time
    C. at the same time
    D. frequently

2. INQUIRE

    A. order
    B. agree
    C. ask
    D. discharge

3. SUFFICIENT

    A. enough
    B. inadequate
    C. thorough
    D. capable

4. AMBULATORY

    A. bedridden
    B. left-handed
    C. walking
    D. laboratory

5. DILATE

    A. enlarge
    B. contract
    C. revise
    D. restrict

6. NUTRITIOUS

    A. protective
    B. healthful
    C. fattening
    D. nourishing

7. CONGENITAL

    A. with pleasure
    B. defective
    C. likeable
    D. existing from birth

8. ISOLATION

    A. sanitation
    B. quarantine
    C. rudeness
    D. exposure

9. SPASM

    A. splash
    B. twitch
    C. space
    D. blow

10. HEMORRHAGE
    A. bleeding   B. ulcer
    C. hereditary disease   D. lack of blood

    10.____

11. NOXIOUS
    A. gaseous   B. harmful   C. soothing   D. repulsive

    11.____

12. PYOGENIC
    A. disease producing   B. fever producing
    C. pus forming   D. water forming

    12.____

13. RENAL
    A. brain   B. heart   C. kidney   D. stomach

    13.____

14. ENDEMIC
    A. epidemic
    B. endermic
    C. endoblast
    D. peculiar to a particular people or locality, as a disease

    14.____

15. MACULATION
    A. reticulation   B. inoculation
    C. maturation   D. defilement

    15.____

16. TOLERATE
    A. fear   B. forgive   C. allow   D. despise

    16.____

17. VENTILATE
    A. vacate   B. air   C. extricate   D. heat

    17.____

18. SUPERIOR
    A. perfect   B. subordinate
    C. lower   D. higher

    18.____

19. EXTREMITY
    A. extent   B. limb   C. illness   D. execution

    19.____

20. DIVULGED
    A. unrefined   B. secreted   C. revealed   D. divided

    20.____

21. SIPHON
    A. drain   B. drink   C. compute   D. discard

    21.____

22. EXPIRATION
    A. trip   B. demonstration
    C. examination   D. end

    22.____

23. AEROSOL 23._____

    A. a gas dispersed in a liquid
    B. a liquid dispersed in a gas
    C. a liquid dispersed in a solid
    D. a solid dispersed in a liquid

24. ETIOLOGY 24._____

    A. cause of a disease   B. method of cure
    C. method of diagnosis   D. study of insects

25. IN VITRO 25._____

    A. in alkali   B. in the body
    C. in the test tube   D. in vacuum

KEY (CORRECT ANSWERS)

1.	B	11.	B
2.	C	12.	C
3.	A	13.	C
4.	C	14.	D
5.	A	15.	D
6.	D	16.	C
7.	D	17.	B
8.	B	18.	D
9.	B	19.	B
10.	A	20.	C

21. A
22. D
23. B
24. A
25. C

CODING
EXAMINATION SECTION

COMMENTARY

An ingenious question-type called coding, involving elements of alphabetizing, filing, name and number comparison, and evaluative judgment and application, has currently won wide acceptance in testing circles for measuring clerical aptitude and general ability, particularly on the senior (middle) grades (levels).

While the directions for this question usually vary in detail, the candidate is generally asked to consider groups of names, codes, and numbers, and then, according to a given plan, to arrange codes in alphabetic order; to arrange these in numerical sequence; to re-arrange columns of names and numbers in correct order; to espy errors in coding; to choose the correct coding arrangement in consonance with the given directions and examples, etc.

This question-type appear to have few parameters in respect to form, substance, or degree of difficulty.

Accordingly, acquaintance with, and practice in, the coding question is recommended for the serious candidate.

TEST 1

DIRECTIONS: Questions 1 through 8 are to be answered on the basis of the code table and the instructions given below.

Code Letter for Traffic Problem	B	H	Q	J	F	L	M	I
Code Number for Action Taken	1	2	3	4	5	6	7	8

Assume that each of the capital letters on the above chart is a radio code for a particular traffic problem and that the number immediately below each capital letter is the radio code for the correct action to be taken to deal with the problem. For instance, "1" is the action to be taken to deal with problem "B", "2" is the action to be taken to deal with problem "H", and so forth.

In each question, a series of code letters is given in Column 1. Column 2 gives four different arrangements of code numbers. You are to pick the answer (A, B, C, or D) in Column 2 that gives the code numbers that match the code letters in the same order.

SAMPLE QUESTION

Column 1
BHLFMQ

Column 2
A. 125678
B. 216573
C. 127653
D. 126573

According to the chart, the code numbers that correspond to these code letters are as follows: B – 1, M – 2, L – 6, F – 5, M – 7, Q – 3. Therefore, the right answer is 126573. This answer is D in Column 2.

2 (#1)

	Column 1		Column 2	

1. BHQLMI
   - A. 123456
   - B. 123567
   - C. 123678
   - D. 125678

   1.____

2. HBJQLF
   - A. 214365
   - B. 213456
   - C. 213465
   - D. 214387

   2.____

3. QHMLFJ
   - A. 321654
   - B. 345678
   - C. 327645
   - D. 327654

   3.____

4. FLQJIM
   - A. 543287
   - B. 563487
   - C. 564378
   - D. 654378

   4.____

5. FBIHMJ
   - A. 518274
   - B. 152874
   - C. 528164
   - D. 517842

   5.____

6. MIHFQB
   - A. 872341
   - B. 782531
   - C. 782341
   - D. 783214

   6.____

7. JLFHQIM
   - A. 465237
   - B. 456387
   - C. 4652387
   - D. 4562387

   7.____

8. LBJQIFH
   - A. 614382
   - B. 6134852
   - C. 61437852
   - D. 61431852

   8.____

KEY (CORRECT ANSWERS)

1. C
2. A
3. D
4. B
5. A
6. B
7. C
8. A

TEST 2

DIRECTIONS: Each question or incomplete statement is followed by several suggested answers or completions. Select the one that BEST answers the question or completes the statement. *PRINT THE LETTER OF THE CORRECT ANSWER IN THE SPACE AT THE RIGHT.*

Questions 1-5.

DIRECTIONS: Questions 1 through 5 are based on the following list showing the name and number of each of nine inmates.

1. Johnson   4. Thompson   7. Gordon
2. Smith   5. Frank   8. Porter
3. Edwards   6. Murray   9. Lopez

Each question consists of 3 sets of numbers and letters. Each set should consist of the numbers of three inmates and the first letter of each of their names. The letters should be in the same order as the numbers. In at least two of the three choices, there will be an error. On your answer sheet, mark only that choice in which the letters correspond with the numbers and are in the same order. If all three sets are wrong, mark choice D in your answer space.

<u>SAMPLE QUESTION</u>
A. 386 EPM
B. 542 FST
C. 474 LGT

Since 3 corresponds to E for Edwards, 8 corresponds to P for Porter, and 6 corresponds to M for Murray, choice A is correct and should be entered in your answer space. Choice B is wrong because letters T and S have been reversed. Choice C is wrong because the first number, which is 4, does NOT correspond with the first letter of choice C, which is L. It should have been T. If choice A were also wrong, then D would be the correct answer.

1. A. 382 EGS   B. 461 TMJ   C. 875 PLF   1._____

2. A. 549 FLT   B. 692 MJS   C. 758 GSP   2._____

3. A. 936 LEM   B. 253 FSE   C. 147 JTL   3._____

4. A. 569 PML   B. 716 GJP   C. 842 PTS   4._____

5. A. 356 FEM   B. 198 JPL   C. 637 MEG   5._____

Questions 6-10.

DIRECTIONS: Questions 6 through 10 are to be answered on the basis of the following information:

2 (#3)

In order to make sure stock is properly located, incoming units are stored as follows:

STOCK NUMBERS	BIN NUMBERS
00100 – 39999	D30, L44
40000 – 69999	14L, D38
70000 – 99999	41L, 80D
100000 and over	614, 83D

Using the above table, choose the answer A, B, C, or D, which lists the correct Bin Number for the Stock Number given.

6. 17243
 A. 41L   B. 83D   C. 14L   D. D30   6.____

7. 9219
 A. D38   B. L44   C. 614   D. 41L   7.____

8. 90125
 A. 41L   B. 614   C. D38   D. D30   8.____

9. 10001
 A. L44   B. D38   C. 80D   D. 83D   9.____

10. 200100
 A. 41L   B. 14L   C. 83D   D. D30   10.____

KEY (CORRECT ANSWERS)

1.	B	6.	D
2.	D	7.	B
3.	A	8.	A
4.	C	9.	A
5.	C	10.	C

TEST 3

DIRECTIONS: Each question or incomplete statement is followed by several suggested answers or completions. Select the one that BEST answers the question or completes the statement. *PRINT THE LETTER OF THE CORRECT ANSWER IN THE SPACE AT THE RIGHT.*

Questions 1-9.

DIRECTIONS: Assume that the Police Department is planning to conduct a statistical study of individuals who have been convicted of crimes during a certain year. For the purpose of this study, identification numbers are being assigned to individuals in the following manner:

The first two digits indicate the age of the individual.
The third digit indicates the sex of the individual:
    1. Male
    2. Female
The fourth digit indicates the type of crime involved:
    1. criminal homicide
    2. forcible rape
    3. robbery
    4. aggravated assault
    5. burglary
    6. larceny
    7. auto theft
    8. other
The fifth and sixth digits indicate the month in which the conviction occurred:
    01. January
    02. February, etc.

Questions 1 through 9 are to be answered SOLELY on the basis of the above information and the following list of individuals and identification numbers.

Abbott, Richard	271304	Morris, Chris	212705
Collins, Terry	352111	Owens, William	231412
Elders, Edward	191207	Parker, Leonard	291807
George, Linda	182809	Robinson, Charles	311102
Hill, Leslie	251702	Sands, Jean	202610
Jones, Jackie	301106	Smith, Michael	42108
Lewis, Edith	402406	Turner, Donald	191601
Mack, Helen	332509	White, Barbara	242803

1. The number of women on the above list is
    A. 6   B. 7   C. 8   D. 9

1.____

2. The two convictions which occurred during February were for the crimes of
    A. aggravated assault and auto theft
    B. auto theft and criminal homicide
    C. burglary and larceny
    D. forcible rape and robbery

3. The ONLY man convicted of auto theft was
    A. Richard Abbott   B. Leslie Hill
    C. Chris Morris   D. Leonard Parker

4. The number of people on the list who were 25 years old or older is
    A. 6   B. 7   C. 8   D. 9

5. The OLDEST person on the list is
    A. Terry Collins   B. Edith Lewis
    C. Helen Mack   D. Michael Smith

6. The two people on the list who are the same age are
    A. Richard Abbott and Michael Smith
    B. Edward Elders and Donald Turner
    C. Linda George and Helen Mack
    D. Leslie Hill and Charles Robinson

7. A 28-year-old man who was convicted of aggravated assault in October would have identification number
    A. 281410   B. 281509   C. 282311   D. 282409

8. A 33-year-old woman convicted in April of criminal homicide would have identification number
    A. 331140   B. 331204   C. 332014   D. 332104

9. The number of people on the above list who were convicted during the first six months of the year is
    A. 6   B. 7   C. 8   D. 9

Questions 10-19.

DIRECTIONS: The following is a list of patients who were referred by various clinics to the laboratory for tests. After each name is a patient identification number. Questions 10 through 19 are to be answered on the basis of the information contained in this list and the explanation accompanying it.

The first digit refers to the clinic which made the referral:
1. cardiac   6. Hematology
2. Renal   7. Gynecology
3. Pediatrics   8. Neurology
4. Ophthalmology   9. Gastroenterology
5. Orthopedics

The second digit refers to the sex of the patient:
  1. male
  2. female
The third and fourth digits give the age of the patient
The last two digits give the day of the month the laboratory tests were performed

LABORATORY REFERRALS DURING JANUARY

Adams, Jacqueline	320917	Miller, Michael	511806
Black, Leslie	813406	Pratt, William	214411
Cook, Marie	511616	Rogers, Ellen	722428
Fisher, Pat	914625	Saunders, Sally	310229
Jackson, Lee	923212	Wilson, Jan	416715
James, Linda	624621	Wyatt, Mark	321326
Lane, Arthur	115702		

10. According to the list, the number of women referred to the laboratory during January was
    A. 4   B. 5   C. 6   D. 7

11. The clinic from which the MOST patients were referred was
    A. Cardiac
    B. Gynecology
    C. Ophthalmology
    D. Pediatrics

12. The YOUNGEST patient referred from any clinic other than Pediatrics was
    A. Leslie Black
    B. Marie Cook
    C. Arthur Lane
    D. Sally Saunders

13. The number of patients whose laboratory tests were performed on or before January 16 was
    A. 7   B. 8   C. 9   D. 10

14. The number of patients referred for laboratory tests who are under age 45 is
    A. 7   B. 8   C. 9   D. 10

15. The OLDEST patient referred to the clinic during January was
    A. Jacqueline Adams
    B. Linda James
    C. Arthur Lane
    D. Jan Wilson

16. The ONLY patient treated in the Orthopedics clinic was
    A. Marie Cook
    B. Pat Fisher
    C. Ellen Rogers
    D. Jan Wilson

17. A woman, age 37 was referred from the Hematology clinic to the laboratory. Her laboratory tests were performed on January 9. Her identification number would be
    A. 610937   B. 623709   C. 613790   D. 623790

18. A man was referred for lab tests from the Orthopedics clinic. He is 30 years old and his tests were performed on January 6.
    His identification number would be
    A. 413006   B. 510360   C. 513006   D. 513060

18.____

19. A 4-year-old boy was referred from the Pediatrics clinic to have laboratory tests on January 23.
    His identification number was
    A. 310422   B. 310423   C. 310433   D. 320403

19.____

KEY (CORRECT ANSWERS)

1.	B	11.	D
2.	B	12.	B
3.	B	13.	A
4.	D	14.	C
5.	D	15.	D
6.	B	16.	A
7.	A	17.	B
8.	D	18.	C
9.	C	19.	B
10.	B		

TEST 4

DIRECTIONS: Each question or incomplete statement is followed by several suggested answers or completions. Select the one that BEST answers the question or completes the statement. *PRINT THE LETTER OF THE CORRECT ANSWER IN THE SPACE AT THE RIGHT.*

Questions 1-10.

DIRECTIONS: Questions 1 through 10 are to be answered on the basis of the information and directions given below.

Assume that you are a Senior Stenographer assigned to the personnel bureau of a city agency. Your supervisor has asked you to classify the employees in your agency into the following five groups:

- A. Employees who are college graduates, who are at least 35 years of age but less than 50, and who have been employed by the City for five years or more;
- B. Employees who have been employed by the City for less than five years, who are not college graduates, and who earn at least $32,500 a year but less than $34,500;
- C. Employees who have been City employees for five years or more, who are at least 21 years of age but less than 35, and who are not college graduates;
- D. Employee who earn at least $34,500 a year but less than $36,000 who are college graduates, and who have been employed by the City for less than five years;
- E. Employees who are not included in any of the foregoing groups.

NOTE: In classifying these employees you are to compute age and period of service as of January 1, 2003. In all cases, it is to be assumed that each employee has been employed continuously in City service. In each question, consider only the information which will assist you in classifying each employee Any information which is of no assistance in classifying an employee would not be considered.

SAMPLE: Mr. Brown, a 29-year-old veteran, was appointed to his present position of Clerk on June 1, 2000. He has completed two years of college. His present salary is $33,050.

The correct answer to this sample is B, since the employee has been employed by the City for less than five years, is not a college graduate, and earn at least $32,500 a year but less than $34,500.

Questions 1 through 10 contain excerpts from the personnel records of 10 employees in the agency. In the correspondingly numbered space at the right print the capital letter preceding the appropriate group into which you would place each employee.

1. Mr. James has been employed by the City since 1993, when he was graduated from a local college. Now 35 years of age, he earns $36,000 a year.

1.____

2. Mr. Worth began working in City service early in 1999. He was awarded his college degree in 1994, at the age of 21. As a result of a recent promotion, he now earns $34,500 a year.

2.____

2 (#4)

3. Miss Thomas has been a City employee since August 1, 1998. Her salary is $34,500 a year. Miss Thomas, who is 25 years old, has had only three years of high school training.

3.____

4. Mr. Williams has had three promotions since entering City service on January 1, 1991. He was graduated from college with honors in 1974, when he was 20 years of age. His present salary is $37,000 a year.

4.____

5. Miss Jones left college after two years of study to take an appointment to a position in the City service paying $33,300 a year. She began work on March 1, 1997 when she was 19 years of age.

5.____

6. Mr. Smith was graduated from an engineering college with honors in January 1998 and became a City employee three months later. His present salary is $35,810. Mr. Smith was born in 1976.

6.____

7. Miss Earnest was born on May 31, 1979. Her education consisted of four years of high school and one year of business school. She was appointed as a typist in a City agency on June 1, 1997. Her annual salary is $33,500.

7.____

8. Mr. Adams, a 24-year-old clerk, began his City service on July 1, 1999, soon after being discharged from the U.S. Army. A college graduate, his present annual salary is $33,200.

8.____

9. Miss Charles attends college in the evenings, hoping to obtain her degree is 2004, when she will be 30 years of age. She has been a City employee since April 1998, and earns $33,350.

9.____

10. Mr. Dolan was just promoted to his present position after six years of City service. He was graduated from high school in 1982, when he was 18 years of age, but did not go on to college. Mr. Dolan's present salary is $33,500.

10.____

KEY (CORRECT ANSWERS)

1.	A	6.	D
2.	D	7.	C
3.	E	8.	E
4.	A	9.	B
5.	C	10.	E

TEST 5

DIRECTIONS: Questions 1 through 4 each contain five numbers that should be arranged in numerical order. The number with the lowest numerical value should be first and the number with the highest numerical value should be last. Pick that option which indicates the CORRECT order of the numbers.

Examples: A. 9; 18; 14; 15; 27
              B. 9; 14; 15; 18; 27
              C. 14; 15; 18; 27; 9
              D. 9; 14; 15; 27; 18

The correct answer is B, which contains the proper arrangement of the five numbers.

1.   A. 20573; 20753; 20738; 20837; 20098
    B. 20098; 20753; 20573; 20738; 20837
    C. 20098; 20573; 20753; 20837; 20738
    D. 20098; 20573; 20738; 20753; 20837

1.____

2.   A. 113492; 113429; 111314; 113114; 131413
    B. 111314; 113114; 113429; 113492; 131413
    C. 111314; 113429; 113492; 113114; 131413
    D. 111314; 113114; 131413; 113429; 113492

2.____

3.   A. 1029763; 1030421; 1035681; 1036928; 1067391
    B. 1030421; 1029763; 1035681; 1067391; 1036928
    C. 1030421; 1035681; 1036928; 1067391; 1029763
    D. 1029763; 1039421; 1035681; 1067391; 1036928

3.____

4.   A. 1112315; 1112326; 1112337; 1112349; 1112306
    B. 1112306; 1112315; 1112337; 1112326; 1112349
    C. 1112306; 1112315; 1112326; 1112337; 1112349
    D. 1112306; 1112326; 1112315; 1112337; 1112349

4.____

KEY (CORRECT ANSWERS)

1. D
2. B
3. A
4. C

TEST 6

DIRECTIONS: The phonetic filing system is a method of filing names in which the alphabet is reduced to key code letters. The six key letters and their equivalents are as follows:

KEY LETTERS	EQUIVALENTS
b	p, f, v
c	s, k, g, j, q, x, z
d	t
l	none
m	n
r	none

A key letter represents itself.
Vowels (a, e, i, o, and u) and the letters w, h, and y are omitted.
For example, the name GILMAN would be represented as follows:
   G is represented by the key letter C.
   I is a vowel and is omitted.
   L is a letter and represents itself.
   M is a key letter and represents itself.
   A is a vowel and is omitted.
   N is represented by the key letter M.

Therefore, the phonetic filing code for the name GILMAN is CLMM.

Answer Questions 1 through 10 based on the information below.

1. The phonetic filing code for the name FITZGERALD would be
   A. BDCCRLD   B. BDCRLD   C. BDZCRLD   D. BTZCRLD

2. The phonetic filing code CLBR may represent any one of the following names EXCEPT
   A. Calprey   B. Flower   C. Glover   D. Silver

3. The phonetic filing code LDM may represent any one of the following names EXCEPT
   A. Halden   B. Hilton   C. Walton   D. Wilson

4. The phonetic filing code for the name RODRIGUEZ would be
   A. RDRC   B. RDRCC   C. RDRCZ   D. RTRCC

5. The phonetic filing code for the name MAXWELL would be
   A. MCLL   B. MCWL   C. MCWLL   D. MXLL

6. The phonetic filing code for the name ANDERSON would be
   A. AMDRCM   B. ENDRSM   C. MDRCM   D. NDERCN

7. The phonetic filing code for the name SAVITSKY would be
   A. CBDCC   B. CBDCY   C. SBDCC   D. SVDCC

8. The phonetic filing code CMC may represent any one of the following names EXCEPT
   A. James   B. Jayes   C. Johns   D. Jones

   8.____

9. The ONLY one of the following names that could be represented by the phonetic filing code CDDDM would be
   A. Catalano   B. Chesterton   C. Cittadino   D. Cuttlerman

   9.____

10. The ONLY one of the following names that could be represented by the phonetic filing code LLMCM would be
    A. Ellington   B. Hallerman   C. Inslerman   D. Willingham

    10.____

KEY (CORRECT ANSWERS)

1. A 6. C
2. B 7. A
3. D 8. B
4. B 9. C
5. A 10. D

GLOSSARY OF ANATOMIC SCIENCES

CONTENTS

	Page
Achilles Tendon .... Concha	1
Costal............................Iliacus	2
Iliocostal........................... Pubis	3
Radius......................... Zygoma	4

GLOSSARY OF ANATOMIC SCIENCES

ACHILLES TENDON
The tendon which attaches to the heel and originates from the muscles in the calf (gastrocnemius and soleus muscles).
ANCONEUS
This muscle extends from humerus in upper forearm to ulna in forearm. Its function is to straighten the elbow joint.
ARYEPIGLOTTIC
From the arytenoid cartilage to the epiglottis (the structure which closes the windpipe when swallowing). Its function is to close entrance to larynx.
ARYTENOID
From one arytenoid cartilage to other, its function is to close the larynx.
ASTRAGALUS
Located just below tibia and fibula (leg bones) in ankle. It connects with the heel bone.
ATLAS
First vertebra lying just beneath the skull.
AXIS
Second vertebra in neck, just below Atlas.

B

BRACHIALIS
Extends from upper and lower jaw bones too muscles about the mouth. Its function is to pull back angles of the mouth and tighten the cheeks.
BULBO-CAVERNOSUS
Extends from perineum (a point below the genitals) to penis. Its function is to compress urethra.

C

CALCANEUS
Heel bone.
CALVARIUM
Bones which form top of skull.
CAPITATE
Largest bone in wrist, located toward center of wrist joint.
CARPAL
Eight small bones of wrist greater multangular, lesser multangular, lunate, capitate, hamate, navicular, triquetrum, and pisiform bones.
CILIARY
Extends from membrane around iris to ciliary process of iris in the eye. Its function is to open and close the pupil of the eye.
CLAVICLE
Collarbone extending from sternum (breastbone) to shoulder tip.
COCCYX
Tailbone, the last vertebrae at base of spine.
CONCHA
Shell-shaped small bone located along the outer side of the nasal cavity.

COSTAL
  Ribs; 12 bones on each side, arising from the spinal column.
COXAE
  Hipbone; joins with sacrum and other hipbone to form the bon pelvis. The Coxae is composed of 3 fused bones: ilium, ischium, and pubis.
CRICOARYTENOID
  From cricoid cartilages to arytenoid cartilages in the neck. It function is to open and close the vocal chords.
CUROID
  Cube-shaped small bone of foot.

D

DELTOID
  Extends from the collarbone and the scapula, over the shoulder, to the humerus in the upper arm. Its function is to lift the upper arm away from the body.

E

ETHMOID
  Small bone located in front of base of skull, forming part of orbit and nose. Within it are spaces, making up the ethmoid sinuses.
EXTENSOR CARPI RADIALIS
  From humerus to bones of wrist. Its function is to straighten the wrist.

F

FEMUR
  The thighbone, extending from hip to knee.
FIBULA
  Outer bone of leg, extending from knee to ankle
FLEXOR CARPI RADIALIS
  Extends from humerus to bones in front of the wrist. Its function is to bend the wrist.
FRONTAL
  Bones of forehead, parts of orbit and nose.

G

GASTROCNEMIUS
  Extends down leg from femur to heel bone. Its function is to bend ankle in downward direction and to help flex knee.

H

HAMSTRING
  Three large muscles extending down back of the thigh from ischium to tibia below the knee. Its function is to flex the knee joint.
HUMERUS
  Arm bone, extending from shoulder to elbow.
HYOID
  Thin U-shaped bone beneath the chin and above the larynx.

ILIACUS
  Extends from pelvis bones to femur in the thigh. Its function is to flex hip joint.

ILIOCOSTAL
From ribs to vertebral column. Its function is to straighten spinal column and bend trunk sideways.
ILLIUM
Part of hipbone, into which the femur fits.
INCUS
The anvil. One of 3 small bones of middle ear, adjacent to eardrum.
ISCHIUM
Part of hipbone

L

LONGISSIMUS
Extends up back near spine. Its function is to straighten spine. LONGUS CAPITIS
Extends from vertebrae in neck to base of the skull. Its function is to flex the head.

M

MALAR
Cheekbone; the zygoma.
MALLEUS
The hammer. One of 3 small bones of middle ear; adjacent to eardrum.
MANDIBLE
Jawbone. Attached to the skull at the temperanandibular joint in front of the ear.
MASSETER
Extends from cheekbone to the lower jawbone. Its function is to close the mouth.
MAXILLA
Upper jawbone. Makes up part of the face, orbit, nose, etc.
METACARPAL
The 5 bones of the hand to which the finger bones are attached.
METATARSAL
The 5 bones of the foot to which the toe bones are attached.

N

NASALIS
Maxillary bone of face to bridge. Alters expression of face.
NAVICULAR
Small bones of the hands and feet; shaped like a boat.

O

OBTURATOR
Extends from bones of pubis to femur (thighbone). Rotates thigh outward.
OCCIPITAL
The back and part of base of the skull.

P

PALMARIS
Extends down front of forearm to palm of the hand. Helps to flex the wrist and make "hollow of the hand."
PARIETAL
This bone makes up part of the side and top of the skull.
PATELLA
The kneecap.
PELVIS
The bony pelvis is made up of the hipbones, sacrum, and coccyx.
PHALANGES
The bones of the fingers and toes.
PUBIS
The bone in front of the pelvis.

R

RADIUS
Long bone on outer side of the forearm, extending from elbow to wrist.

S

SACRUM
Five fused vertebrae in lower back which make up the back part of the bony pelvis.

SCALENE
Extends from vertebra in the neck to the first and second ribs. Bends the head and neck sideways.

SCAPULA
The shoulder blade (wing bone).

SPHENOID
Irregularly shaped bone making up front portion of the base of the skull and parts of the orbit and nose.

SPLENIUS
Extends from the vertebrae in the chest and the neck to back of the head. Straightens the head and spine.

STAPES
The stirrup. One of 3 small bones of middle ear adjacent to the eardrum.

STERNUM
The breastbone.

T

TALUS
The same as the astragalus.

TARSAL
The same as the foot bones.

TEMPORAL
The bone forming front portion of the side of the skull and part of the base. Extends from temple to lower jaw. Closes the mouth.

TIBIA
The large inner bone of the leg, extending from knee to the ankle (It is responsible for weight bearing.)

TURBINATE
Three bones located on the outer side of the nasal cavity.

U

ULNA
The long bone on the inner side of the forearm, extending from the elbow to the wrist.

V

VASTUS
It extends down the entire front of the thigh to the kneecap and tibia in the leg its function is to straighten the knee.

VOMER
This bone forms the back segment of the nasal septum which separates the two side of the nose

Z

ZYGOMA
The cheekbone; the malar bone.

GLOSSARY OF MEDICAL TERMS

CONTENTS

		Page
Abduction	Arteriosclerosis	1
Artery	Biceps Muscle	2
Bifida	Causalgia	3
Cullulitis	Colon	4
Comminuted	Dermaphytosis	5
Desiccation	Dysuria	6
Ecchymosis	Epigastric	7
Epilepsy, Jacksonian	Fascia	8
Felon	Genito-Urinary	9
Genu	Herniotomy	10
Humerus	Intertrochanteric	11
Intervertebral	Leucocytosis	12
Leucopenia	Metabolism	13
Metacarpus	Neuroma	14
Neuropsychiatric	Orthopnea	15
Os	Paraplegia	16
Paravertebral	Periosteum	17
Periphery	Pneumonia	18
Pneumonoconiosis	Pyelogram	19
Pyogenic	Scaphoid	20
Scapula	Supinate	21
Suture	Tibia	22
Tinnitus	Ununited	23
Ureter	Zygoma	24

GLOSSARY OF MEDICAL TERMS

A

Abduction
Movement of limb away from middle line of the body.
Abrasion
A scraping away of a portion of the skin.
Abscess
Localized collection of pus or matter.
Acetabulum
Cup-shaped depression on external surface of the pelvic bone (innominate) into which the head of femur, or thighbone, fits.
Achilles Reflex
Movement of foot downward when the tendon immediately above the heel bone is struck.
Acromion
Process of bone constituting tip of shoulder.
Adduction
Movement of limb toward middle line of body.
Adhesion
The matting together of two surfaces by inflammation.
Alae Nash
Outer flaring walls of the nostrils.
Allergic
Reaction of tissues of the body to a protein substance to which the body is especially sensitive.
Anemia
A condition in which the red blood cells and/or hemoglobin are reduced.
Aneurysm
Sac, filled with blood, formed by the local dilation of walls of artery.
Angina Pectoris
Pain in chest associated with heart disease.
Ankyloses
Complete absence of motion at a joint.
Anterior
The anatomical "front" of the body.
Aorta
Main trunk of the systemic arterial system, arising from base of left ventricle.
Apex
Extremity of conical or pyramidal structure, such as heart or lung.
Aphasia
Loss of power of speech by damage to speech center.
Apoplexy
Another word for stroke.
Arrhythmia
Loss of normal rhythm of the heart.
Arteriosclerosis
Hardening of the arteries.

Artery
   Blood vessel conveying blood away from the heart to different parts of the body.
Arthritis
   Inflammation of a joint.
Arthrodesis
   Stiffening of a joint.
Articulation
   Joint.
Asbestosis
   Dust disease of asbestos workers.
Aseptic
   Free of germs.
Aspiration
   Withdrawal, by suction, of air or fluid from any cavity.
Asthma
   Disease marked by recurrent attacks of shortness, of breath, due to temporary change in bronchial tubes, making person uncomfortable.
Astigmatism
   An abnormality in the curve of the 'anterior visual surface of the eyeball.
Astragalus
   One of the ankle bones.
Ataxia
   Disturbance of coordination of muscular movements.
Atelectasis
   Collapse of lung tissue due to failure of entrance of air into air-cells.
Atrophy
   Wasting or diminution in size of a structure.
Audiogram
   Graphic record made by an audiometer, an electrical instrument for recording acuity of hearing.
Auricular fibrillation
   Irregular beat as to time and force beginning in auricle of the heart.
Auscultation
   The act of listening to sounds within the body.
Axillary
   Relating to armpit.

B

Baker's Cyst
   Enlargement of synovial sac in the back of the knee joint.
Basal Metabolism
   The energy expended for the absolute minimum requirements of the body at complete rest.
Bell's Palsy
   A form of facial paralysis.
Benign
   Not malignant.
Biceps Muscle
   A muscle over front of arm.

Bifida
>Split or cleft.

Bilateral
>Relating to or having two sides.

Blood Pressure
>Pressure or tension of the blood within the arteries.

Brachial
>Pertaining to the arm.

Bradycardia
>Abnormal slowness of the heartbeat.

Brain
>Mass of nerve tissue which is contained within the skull.

Bronchiectasis
>Dilation of the narrowest portions of the breathing tubes of the lung.

Bronchitis
>Inflammation of mucus membrane of bronchial tubes.

Buerger's Disease
>Thromboangiitis obliterans; obliteration and inflammation of the larger arteries and veins of a limb by clotting and inflammation, involving nerve trunks.

Bursa
>A lubricating sac usually found at pressure points or around joints.

Bursitis
>Inflammation of the bursa.

C

Calcaneum
>The os calcis, or heel bone.

Calcification
>X-ray opaque substance found in serious tissues of the body.

Canthus
>Either extremity of the slit between the eyelids.

Capitellum
>Portion of bone found at the end of the arm bone.

Capsule
>Fibrous membrane which envelopes an organ, joint or a foreign body.

Carbuncle
>Group of boils resulting in localized gangrene or death of affected tissues.

Cardiac
>Pertaining to the heart.

Cardiologist
>Heart specialist.

Catheter
>Hollow cylinder of silver, India rubber or other material, designed to be passed into a hollow area for drainage purposes.

Cartilage
>White substance which covers ends of bones.

Causalgia
>A painful condition.

Cellulitis
   Diffuse inflammation of cellular tissue, i.e., especially loose cellular tissue just underneath skin.
Cephalalgia
   Headache.
Cerebellum
   Back part of the brain, concerned in coordination of movements.
Cerebrum
   Front part of the brain, concerned with the conscious processes of the mind.
Cervix
   Neck or neck-like part.
Charcot's joint
   Painless joint destruction.
Cholecystectomy
   Surgical removal of the gall-bladder.
Cholecystis
   Inflammation of gall-bladder.
Cholelithiasis
   Gallstone.
Chorio-Retinal
   Relating to the visual tissue of eye and its supporting structure.
Chondral
   Pertaining to cartilage.
Cicatrix
   Scar.
Cirrhosis
   Fibrosis or sclerosis of any organ; hardening.
Clavicle
   Collar bone.
Clonus
   Muscular spasm in which contraction and relaxation of muscle follow one another in rapid succession.
Coccydynia
   Pain in the coccyx.
Coccygectomy
   Removal of the coccyx.
Coccygeal
   Relating to the coccyx.
Coccyx
   Small bone at the end of the spinal column in man.
Congenital
   Existing at birth.
Congestion
   Engorgement of blood vessels of a part.
Conjunctiva
   Delicate membrane which lines the inner surface of the eyelids and covers the eyeball in front.
Colles Fracture
   Fracture of lower end of radius
Colon
   The last part of the intestinal tract.

Comminuted
  Broken into more than two fragments.
Concussion
  Injury of a soft structure, as the brain, resulting from a blow or violent shaking.
Coronary Artery
  The artery providing nutrition to the heart muscle.
Cornea
  Transparent structure forming the anterior part of the external layer of eyeball.
Cortex
  Outer portion of an organ, such as the kidney, as distinguished from inner or medullary portion; external layer of gray matter covering hemispheres of cerebrum and cerebellum.
Costal
  Pertaining to the ribs.
Coxa
  Hip joint.
Cranium
  Skull.
Crepitus
  Abnormal sounds heard in the case of fractured bones and diseased tissues when rubbing together.
Curettage
  Scraping the interior of a cavity for the removal of tissue.
Cutaneous
  Relating to the skin.
Cyanosis
  Blueish discoloration of external tissue, e.g. lips, nails, skin.
Cyst
  Abnormal sac which contains a liquid or semi-solid.
Cystoscopy
  Inspection of the interior of the bladder with a cystoscope.
Cystostomy
  Formation of a more or less permanent opening into the urinary bladder.

D

Dactyl
  Digit: Finger or toe.
Decompensation
  Failure to maintain normal function as in heart failure.
Deltoid
  Triangular-shaped muscle of the shoulder.
Dementia
  Form of insanity.
Dermatitis
  Inflammation of the skin.
Dermatologist
  Skin specialist.
Dermaphytosis
  Skin disease due to presence of a vegetable microparasite.

Desiccation
   The removal of tissue by chemical, physical, electrical, freezing, or x-ray.
Diabetes (Melitus)
   A disease having symptoms of excessive urine and sugar excretion.
Diaphragm
   Muscular partition between thorax and abdomen.
Diarrhea
   Abnormally frequent discharge of fluid fecal matter from the bowel.
Diastasis
   Simple separation of normally joined parts.
Diastole
   Period of rest during which heart is filling up for next beat.
Diathermy
   Local elevation of temperature in tissues, produced by special form of high-frequency current.
Diathesis
   Predisposition to a disease.
Digit
   Finger or toe.
Dilatation
   Enlargement, due to stretching or thinning out of tissues.
Diplopia
   Double-vision.
Disc
   A round flat surface variously found in eye and spinal column conditions.
Dislocation
   Most frequently used in orthopedics to describe a disturbance of normal relationship of bones which enter into formation of a joint.
Distal
   Farthest from the point of origin; the term is usually used in connection with the extremities.
Diverticulum
   Pouch or sac opening out from a tubular organ.
Dorsal
   Relating to the back; posterior.
Dorsum
   The back; upper or posterior surface or back of any part.
Duct
   Tube or passage with well-defined walls for passing excretions or secretions.
Duodenum
   Upper portion of intestinal tube connecting with stomach.
Dupuytren's Contraction
   Contraction of the palmar fascia causing permanent flexion of one or more fingers.
Dura Mater
   Outermost and toughest of three membranes covering brain and spinal cord.
Dysphagia
   Difficulty in swallowing.
Dyspnoea
   Difficulty in breathing.
Dysuria
   Difficulty or pain in urination.

E

Ecchymosis
    Black and blue spot on the skin.
Ectropion
    A rolling outward of the margin of an eyelid.
Eczema
    A form of dermatitis.
Edema
    Swelling due to watery effusion in the intercellular spaces.
Electrocardiogram
    Graph of electric currents in the heart.
Electrocardiograph
    Instrument for producing electrocardiogram.
Embolus
    Clot or plug brought by blood-current from distant part.
Embolism
    The plugging up of a blood vessel by a floating mass.
Eminence
    Circumscribed area raised above general area of surrounding surface.
Emphysema
    Abnormal distention with loss of elasticity of the air sacs of the lung.
Empyema
    Accumulation of pus or matter in normally closed cavity on the surface of the lung.
Encephalitis
    Inflammation of the brain substance.
Encephalogram
    Roentgenogram of contents of the skull.
Encephalopathy
    Conditions of disease of the brain.
Endocrine Gland
    A gland which furnishes internal secretion.
Endogenous
    Originating or produced within organism or one of its parts.
Enophthalmos
    Recession of the eyeball within the orbit.
Epicardium
    Cover of the heart.
Epicondyle
    Projection from long bone near articular extremity above or upon condyle.
Epidermis
    Outermost layer of the skin.
Epididymis
    Oblong or boat-shaped body located on back of testicle.
Epidural
    Upon the outer envelope of the brain.
Epigastric
    Depression at pit of abdominal wall at tip of sword-shaped cartilage of sternum.

Epilepsy, Jacksonian
　Convulsive contractions affecting localized groups of muscles without disturbance of mentality.
Epiphysis
　Ends of long bones.
Epistaxis
　Bloody nose.
Epithelium
　Covering of skin and mucus membrane consisting of epithelial cells.
Epithelioma
　Cancer of the skin or mucus membrane.
Erector spinae
　Muscle keeping the spine erects.
Eruption
　A breaking out; redness, spotting or other visible phenomena on the skin or mucus membrane.
Erythema
　Abnormal redness of the skin.
Esophagus
　Gullet. Tube connecting mouth to stomach.
Etiology
　Cause.
Eversion
　A turning outward, as of the eyelid or foot.
Exacerbation
　Increase in severity of disease or symptoms.
Excision
　Operative removal of a portion of an organ.
Excrescence
　Outgrowth from the surface, especially a pathological growth.
Exogenous
　Originating or produced outside.
Exophthalmus
　Protrusion or prominence of the eyeball.
Exostosis
　Bony tumor springing from surface of a bone, most commonly seen at muscular attachments.
Extensor
　A muscle the contraction of which tends to straighten a limb.
Extrasystole
　Premature contraction of one or more heart chambers.
Exudate
　A fluid, often coagulable, extravasated into tissue or cavity.

F

Facies
　Face, countenance, expression; surface.
Fascia
　Sheet or band of fibrous tissue.

Felon
>Abscess in terminal phalanx of a finger.

Femoral
>Relating to the femur or thigh.

Femur
>Thigh bone.

Fibrillation
>Totally irregular beat.

Fibroma
>Fibroid tumor.

Fibrosis
>Pathological formation of fibrous tissue.

Fibula
>Smaller calf bone.

Fistula
>Abnormal passageway leading to surface of body.

Flexion
>Bending of a joint.

Flexor
>A muscle the action of which is to flex a joint.

Follicle
>Very small excretory or secretory sac or gland.

Foramen
>Aperture through a bone or membranous structure.

Fracture, Comminuted
>Bone broken into more than two pieces.

Fracture, Ununited
>One in which union fails to occur.

Frontal
>Relating to the front of body.

Fundus
>Base of a hollow organ.

Fusiform
>Spindle-shaped, tapering at both ends.

G

Ganglion
>Usually used to describe a cystic tumor occurring on a tendon sheath or in connection with a joint.

Gangrene
>Death or masse of any part of the body.

Gastric
>Pertaining to the stomach.

Gastrocnemius
>One of the calf muscles.

Genitalia
>Organs of reproduction.

Genito-Urinary
>Relation to reproduction and urination, noting organs concerned.

Genu
>Knee
Genu-Valgum
>Knock-knee.
Gladiolus
>Middle and largest division of sternum (chest bone).
Gland
>Secreting organ.
Glaucoma
>Increased pressure in the eyeball.
Gluteal
>Pertaining to the buttocks.
Greenstick Fracture
>Incomplete fracture.
Gynecologist
>Specialist in the treatment of diseases peculiar to women.

H

Hallux
>Great toe.
Hallux valgus
>Deviation of great toe toward inner or lateral side of the foot (bunion).
Haematemesis
>Vomiting of blood.
Haemoglobin
>Coloring matter of blood in red blood corpuscles.
Haemoptysis
>Discharge of blood from the lungs by coughing.
Hemarthrosis
>Effusion of blood into cavity of a joint.
Hematoma
>Swelling formed by effused blood.
Hematuria
>Passage of blood in the urine.
Hemianopsia
>Loss of vision for one-half of visual field.
Hemorrhage
>Bleeding, especially if profuse.
Hemorrhoids
>Piles, a varicose condition causing painful swellings of the anus.
Hepatic
>Pertaining to the liver.
Herania
>Protrusion of organ outside of its normal confines.
Hernioplasty
>Operation for hernia.
Herniotomy
>Operation for relief of hernia.

Humerus
    Bone of the upper arm.
Hydrarthrosis
    Effusion of a serous fluid into a joint cavity.
Hydrocele
    Circumscribed collection of fluid around the testicle.
Hydrone Phrosis
    Dilatation inside kidney due to obstruction of flow of urine.
Hyperaesthesia
    Excessive sensitiveness of the skin to touch or hypersensitiveness of any special sense.
Hyperglycaemia
    Abnormally large proportion of sugar in blood.
Hypertension
    High blood pressure often associated with arteriosclerosis.
Hyperthrophy
    Enlargement, general increase in bulk of a part or organ, not due to tumor formation.
Hypogastrium
    Lower middle region of the abdomen.
Hypoplasia
    Under-development of structure.
Hypothenar
    Fleshy mass at the inner (little finger) side of the palm.
Hysteria
    A functional nervous condition characterized by lack of emotional control and sudden temporary attacks of mental, emotional or physical aberration.

I

Ileum
    Portion of the small intestine.
Ilium
    One of the bones of the pelvis.
Impacted
    Driven in firmly.
Incontinence
    Inability to retain a natural discharge.
Induration
    Hardening; spot or area of hardened tissue
Infarct
    Death of tissue due to lack of blood supply
Inguinal
    Relating to the groin.
In situ
    In position.
Intercostal
    Between the ribs
Interstitial
    Relating to spaces within any structure.
Intertrochanteric
    Between the two trochanters of the femur or thigh bone

Intervertebral
    Between two vertebrae.
Iris
    Circular colored portion of the eye which surrounds pupil
Ischaemia
    Local and temporary deficiency of blood.
Ischium
    One of the pelvic bones.

J

Jaundice
    Yellowness of tissues due to absorption of bile.
Jejunum
    Portion of small intestine about 8 feet long, between duodenum and ileum.

K

Kienboeck Disease
    Increased porosity and softness of certain carpal bones.
Keloid
    Peculiar overgrowth of hyaline connective tissues in the skin of predisposed individuals after injury or scarring.
Keratitis
    Inflammation of the cornea.
Kyphosis
    Curvature of the spine, hump-back, hunch-back.

L

Laceration
    Separation of tissue (cut).
Lacriminal
    Relating to the tears apparatus.
Laminae
    Flattened portions of the sides of a vertebral arch.
Laminectomy
    Removal of one or more laminae from the vertebrae.
Larynx
    Organ of voice production.
Lesion
    Any hurt, wound or degeneration.
Leucocytosis
    Temporary increase in relative number of white blood cells in the blood.

Leucopenia
Abnormal decrease in number of white blood corpuscles.
Ligament
Tough fibrous band which connects one bone with another.
Lipoma
Tumor composed of fatty tissue.
Lordosis
Anteroposterior curvature of the spine (opposite to kyphosis).
Lue tic
Syphilitic.
Lumbar
Lower back.
Lumbar Vertebrae
The five vertebrae between the thoracic vertebrae and the sacrum.
Luxation
Dislocation.
Lymphangitis
Inflammation of the lymphatic vessels.

M

Malar
Relating to the cheek-bone.
Malignant
Resistant to treatment; occurring in severe form; tending to grow worse and (in the case of a tumor) to recur after removal. Usually indicates poor end result.
Malleoli
Rounded bony prominences on both sides of the ankle joint.
Mandible
Lower jaw.
Manubrium
Upper portion of the sternum.
Mastectomy
Amputation of the breast.
Maxilla
Upper jaw.
Meatus
Passage or opening.
Meninges
Membranes, specifically the envelope of brain and spinal cord.
Meningitis
Inflammation of the meninges.
Meniscus
Intraarticular fibrocartilage of crescentic or discoid shape found in certain joints.
Mesentery
Web or membrane connecting bowel tube to posterior abdominal wall (a portion of the peritoneum).
Metabolism
The total operation of building up and breaking down tissues.

Metacarpus
Part of hand between wrist and fingers; palm; five metacarpal bones collectively which form skeleton of this part.
Metastasis
Transfer of disease, usually malignant, to remote part of the body.
Metatarsalgia
Pain in the region of the metatarsus(or ball of foot).
Metatarsus
Anterior portion of foot between instep and toes, having as its skeleton five long bones articulating anteriorly with the phalanges.
Mottling
Spotting with patches of varying shades of colors.
Mucocutaneous
Relating to mucus membrane and skin, noting the line of junction of the two at the nasal, oral, vaginal and anal orifices.
Musculature
Arrangement of muscles in a part or in the body as a whole.
Myalgia
Muscular pain.
Myelitis
Inflammation of the substance of the spinal cord.
Myelograph
X-ray picture of spinal cord using radio-opaque substance.
Myocardium
Heart Muscle.
Myocarditis
Inflammation of the muscular walls of the heart.
Myositis
Inflammation of a muscle.

N

Navicular
Boat-shaped, noting a bone in the wrist and one in the ankle.
Nausea
Sickness at the stomach; inclination to vomit.
Nephritis
Inflammation of the kidney.
Necrosis
Death en masse of a portion of tissue.
Nephrosis
Non-inflammatory disease of the kidney.
Neuralgia
Pain radiating along a nerve.
Neuritis
Inflammation of a nerve.
Neurologist
Nerve specialist.
Neuroma
Tumor made up largely of nerve tissue.

Neuropsychiatric
　　Relating to disease of both mind and nervous system.
Neurosis
　　Functional derangement of the nervous system.
Nocturia
　　Bed-wetting.
Node
　　Knob; circumscribed swelling; circumscribed mass of differentiated tissue; knuckle.
Nucleus Pulposus
　　Gelatinous center of an intervertebral disc.
Nystagmus
　　Continuous movement of the eyeballs in the horizontal or vertical plains.

O

Occipital
　　Relating to the back of the head.
Occlude
　　To close up or fit together.
Occular
　　Relating to the eye; visual.
Occult
　　Hidden; concealed, noting a concealed hemorrhage, the blood being so changed as not to be readily recognized.
Olecranon
　　Tip of the elbow.
Omentum
　　Web or apron-like membranous structure lying in front of the intestines.
Opacities
　　Areas lacking in transparency.
Opthalmia
　　Disease of the eye.
Opthalmologist
　　Specialist in eye diseases and refractive errors of the eye.
Optic
　　Relating to the eye or to vision.
Optometrist
　　Person without medical training who fits glasses to correct visual defects.
Orbit
　　Eye-socket.
Orchitis
　　Inflammation of the testicle.
Orchidectomy
　　Castration; removal of one or both testicles.
Orthopedics
　　Branch of surgery which has to do with treatment of diseases of joints and spine and correction of deformities.
Orthopnea
　　Ability to breathe with comfort only when sitting erect or standing.

Os
    Bone
Oscalcis
    Heel-bone.
Ossification
    Formation of bone; change into bone.
Osteoma
    Bone tumor.
Osteomyelitis
    Inflammation of bone and bone marrow.
Osteoporosis
    Disease of bone marked by increased porosity and softness ("thinning" of bone).
Osteotomy
    Cutting a bone, usually by saw or chisel, for removal of a piece of dead bone, correction of knock-knee or other deformity, or for any purpose whatsoever.
Otologist
    Specialist in diseases of the ear.

P

Paget's Disease
    Usually refers to a bone disease.
Pancreas
    Abdominal digestive gland, extending from duodenum to spleen, containing insulin forming cells.
Palate
    Roof of the mouth.
Palliative
    Mitigating; reducing in severity, noting a method of treating a disease or its symptoms.
Palmar
    Referring to the palm of the hand.
Palpate
    To examine by feeling and pressing with the palms and fingers.
Palpebral
    Relating to an, eyelid or the eyelids.
Papule
    Pimple.
Palsy
    Paralysis.
Paraesthesia
    Abnormal spontaneous sensation, such as a burning, pricking, numbness.
Paralysis
    Loss of power of motion.
Paralysis Agitans
    Shaking paralysis, Parkinson's Disease.
Paraplegia
    Paralysis of legs and lower parts of the body.

Paravertebral
Alongside a vertebra or the spinal column.
Parenchymal
Relating to the specific tissue of a gland or organ.
Paresis
Incomplete paralysis.
Parietal
Pertaining to the walls.
Parkinson's Syndrome
Aggregate symptoms, including raised eyebrows and expressionless face, of paralysis agitans.
Paronychia
Inflammation of structures surrounding the nail or the bone itself of finger or toe.
Paralysis Agitans
Shaking paralysis, Parkinson's Disease.
Paraplegia
Paralysis of legs and lower parts of the body.
Paravertebral
Alongside a vertebra or the spinal column.
Parenchymal
Relating to the specific tissue of a gland or organ.
Paresis
Incomplete paralysis.
Parietal
Pertaining to the walls.
Parkinson's Syndrome
Aggregate symptoms, including raised eyebrows and expressionless face, of paralysis agitans.
Paronychia
Inflammation of structures surrounding the nail or the bone itself of finger or toe.
Passive
Not active.
Past-Pointing
Test of integrity of vestibular apparatus of the ear by rotating person in revolving chair.
Patella
Knee-cap.
Pathology
Branch of medicine which treats of the abnormal tissues in disease.
Pectoral
Relating to the chest.
Pedicle
Stalk or stem forming the attachment of a tumor which is non-sessile, i.e., which does not have a broad base of attachment.
Pellegrini, Stieda's Disease
Bony growth over the internal condyle of the femur, a sequel of stieda's fracture.
Pendulous
Hanging freely or loosely.
Pericardium
Sac enveloping the heart.
Periosteum
Thick, fibrous membrane covering the entire surface of a bone.

Periphery
Outer part or surface.
Peristalsis
Worm-like movement of the gastro-intestinal tract.
Peritoneum
Serous membrane which covers abdominal organs and inner aspect of abdominal walls.
Peritonitis
Inflammation of the peritoneum.
Peroneal
Pertaining to the outer aspects of the leg.
Pes
Foot; foot-like or basal structure or part.
Pes Cavus
Exaggeration of the normal arch of the foot; hollowfoot.
Pes Equinus
Permanent extension of the foot so that only the ball rests on the ground.
Petechial
Relating to minute hemorrhagic spots, of pinpoint to pinhead size, in the skin.
Phalanx
Bone of a finger or toe.
Phlebitis
Inflammation of the veins.
Physiology
Science which treats of functions of different parts of the body.
Physiotherapy
Use of natural forces in the treatment of disease, as in electro-hydro, and aero-therapy, massage, and therapeutic exercises, and use of mechanical devices in mechanotherapy.
Pill-RollingTremor
Tremor in paralysis agitans in the form of circular movement of opposed tips of thumb and index finger.
Pilonidal Cyst
Cyst at the lower end of the spine.
Pisiform
Pea-shaped or pea-sized.
Plantar
Relating to the sole of the foot.
Pleura
Serous membrane which invests lungs and covers inner part of the chest walls (similar to peritoneum in abdominal cavity.)
Pleurisy
Inflammation of the pleura.
Plexus
Network or tangle of nerves.
Plumbism
Lead poisoning.
Pneumoconiosis
Dust disease of the lungs.
Pneumonia
Inflammation of lung substance.

Pneumonoconiosis
   Fibrous hardening of the lungs due to irritation caused by inhalation of dust incident to various occupations.
Pneumothorax
   Presence of air or gas in the pleural cavity.

Poliomyelitis
   Inflammation of the anterior portion of the spinal cord.
Polyp
   Pedunculated swelling or outgrowth from a mucus membrane.
Polyuria
   Excessive excretion of urine.
Popliteal
   Relating to the posterior surface of the knee.
Precordium
   Anterior surface of lower part of the thorax.
Pretibial
   Relating to anterior portion of the leg.
Proliferative
   Excess growth.
Pronate
   To rotate the forearm in such a way that the palm of the hand looks backward when the arm is in the anatomical position, or downward when the arm is extended at a right angle with the body.
Prostate
   Gland surrounding neck of the male bladder.
Prostatectomy
   Removal of all or part of the prostate.
Protuberance
   Outgrowth: swelling; knob.
Proximal
   Nearest the trunk or point of origin, said of part of an extremity, artery or nerve so situated.
Psychiatrist
   Alienist; one who specializes in diseases of the mind.
Psychogenic
   Of mental origin or causation.
Ptosis
   Drooping down of an eyelid or an organ.
Pubic
   One of the bones of the pelvis.
Pulmonic
   Relating to the lungs.
Puritis
   Itching irritation.
Purulent
   Having the appearance of pus or matter.
Pyelitis
   Inflammation of a portion of the kidney.
Pyelogram
   Roentgenogram of the area of the kidneys and ureter, by use of opaque substances.

Pyogenic
 Pus-forming.

R

Radiologist
 One skilled in the diagnostic and therapeutic use of x-rays.
Radius
 Outer and shorter of the two bones of forearm.
Rales
 Sounds of varied character heard on auscultation of the chest in cases of disease of the lungs or bronchi.
Rectum
 Terminal portion of the digestive tube.
Reflex
 Involuntary or reflected action or movement.
Renal
 Pertaining to the kidney.
Resection
 Removal of articular ends of one or both bones forming a joint, or of a segment of any part, such as the intestine.
Respiration
 Function common to all living plants or animals, consisting in taking in of oxygen and throwing off products of oxidation in the tissues, mainly carbon dioxide and water.
Retina
 Inner, nervous tunic of the eyeball, consisting of an outer pigment layer and an inner layer formed by expansion of the optic nerve.
Retrosternal
 Behind the sternum.
Rib
 One of twenty-four elongated curved bones forming the main portion of bony wall of the chest.
Rhinitis
 Inflammation of the nasal mucus membrane.
Roentgenologist
 One skilled in the diagnostic and therapeutic use of x-rays.

S

Sacroiliac
 Relating to sacrum and ilium, noting articulation between the two bones and associated ligaments.
Sacrum
 Triangular bone at the base of the spine.
Sarcoma
 Malignant tumor of fibrous tissue or its derivatives.
Scaphoid
 Boat-shaped; hollowed.

Scapula
    Shoulder-blade.
Sciatica
    Painful affection of the sciatic nerve.
Sclerosis
    Hardness
Scoliosis
    Lateral curvature of the spine.
Scrotum
    Sac containing testes.
Semilunar Cartilages
    Two intraarticular fibrocartilages of the knee-joint.
Senile
    Relating to or characteristic of old age.
Septicemia
    Morbid condition due to presence of septic microbes and their poisons in the blood.
Sequela
    Morbid condition following as a consequence of another disease.
Sesamoid.
    Resembling in size or shape a grain of sesame.
Sequestrum
    Piece of dead bone separated from living bone.
Shock
    Sudden vital depression due to injury or emotion which makes an untoward depression.
Siderosis
    Form of dust disease due to presence of iron dust.
Silicosis
    Form of dust disease due to inhalation of stone dust.
Sinusitis
    Inflammation of the lining membrane of any sinus, especially of one of the accessory sinuses of the nose.
Spasm
    Sudden violent involuntary rigid contraction, due to muscular action.
Sphincter
    Orbicular muscle which, when in state of normal contraction, closes one of the orifices of the body.
Spina Bifida
    Limited defect in the spinal column consisting in absence of vertebral arches, through which defect spinal membranes protrude.
Spondylolisthesis
    Forward subluxation of body of vertebra on vertebra below it or on sacrum.
Sprain
    Wrenching of a joint.
Stenosis
    Narrowing of an orifice.
Sternoclavicular
    Relating to sternum and clavicle, noting an articulation and occasional muscle.
Stricture
    Abnormal narrowing of a channel.
Supinate
    To turn forearm and hand volar side uppermost.

Suture
Stitch.
Symphysis
Union between two bones by means of fibrocartilage.
Syncope
Fainting.
Syndrome
Complex of symptoms which occur together.
Synovitis
Inflammation of synovial membrane, especially of a joint.
Systole
Period of the heart-beat during which the heart is contracting.

T

Tachycardia
Abnormal increase in rate of the hearts beat, not subsiding on rest, sudden in onset and offset.
Tarsus
Root of the foot or instep.
Temporamandibular
Relating to the temporal bone (bone of the temple) and lower jaw, noting the articulation of the lower jaw.
Tendon
Inelastic fibrous cord or band in which muscle fibers ends and by which muscle is attached to bone or other structure.
Tendosynovitis
Inflammation of the sheath of a tendon.
Tetanus
Lockjaw.
Thorax
Chest, upper part of the trunk between neck and abdomen; it is formed by the twelve dorsal vertebrae, the twelve pairs of ribs, sternum, and muscles and fascias attached to these; it is separated from the abdomen by the diaphragm; it contains chief organs of circulatory and respiratory systems.
Thrombo Angitis Obliterans
Buerger's disease; obliteration of the larger arteries and veins of a limb by thrombi, with subsequent gangrene. See Buerger's Disease.
Thrombophlebitis
Thrombosis with inflammation of the veins.
Thrombosis
Formation of a clot of blood within a blood vessel.
Thyroid
Gland and cartilage of the larynx.
Thyroidectomy
Removal of the thyroid gland.
Tibia
Shin-bone; inner and larger of two bones of the leg.

Tinnitus
　　Subjective noises (ringing, whistling, booming, etc.) in the ears.
Tonsillitis
　　Inflammation of a tonsil.
Torticollis
　　Wry-neck; stiff-neck; spasmodic contraction of muscles of the neck; the head is drawn to one side and usually rotated so that the chin points the other side.
Torsion
　　Twisting or rotation of a part upon its axis; twisting the cut end of an artery to arrest hemmorhage.
Toxemia
　　Blood-poisoning.
Toxin
　　Poison.
Trachea
　　Windpipe.
Transillumination
　　Shining light through a translucent part to see if fluid is present.
Trapezius
　　Muscle extending from back of the head to shoulderbiade; it moves head and shoulder.
Trauma
　　Wound; injury inflicted usually more or less suddenly by physical agent.
Tremor
　　Trembling, shaking, loss of equilibrium.
Trephine
　　Cylindrical or crown saw used for removal of a disc of bone, especially from the skull, or of other firm tissue as that of the cornea.
Triceps
　　Three-headed muscle extending the forearm. (Covers posterior of upper arm).
Trochanter
　　One of two bony prominences developed from independent osseous centers near the upper extremity of the thigh bone.
Tubercle
　　Circumscribed, rounded, solid elevation on the skin, mucus membrane, or surface of an organ; lesion of tuberculosis consisting of a small isolated nodule or aggregation of nodules.
Tuberosity
　　Broad eminence of bone.

U

Ulcer
　　Open sore other than a wound.
Ulna
　　Inner and larger of the two bones of the forearm.
Umbilicus
　　Navel.
Ununited
　　Not united or knit, noting an unhealed fracture.

Ureter
  Musculomembranous tube leading from kidney to bladder.
Urethra
  Membranous tube leading from bladder to external exit.
Urination
  The passing of urine.
Urogram
  Roentgenogram of any part (kidneys, ureters, bladder) of the urinary tract, with the use of opaque substances.
Urologist
  One versed in the branch of medical science which has to do with urine and its modifications in disease.
Urtcaria
  Hives.
Uterus
  Womb.

V

Varicocele
  Varicose veins of the spermatic cord.
Varicose
  Dilated, as used in reference to veins.
Varix
  Enlarged and tortuous vein, artery, or lymphatic vessel.
Vas
  Vessel.
Vasomotor
  Regulating mechanism controlling expansion and contraction of blood vessels.
Ventral
  Relating to anterior portion.
Ventricular
  Relating to a ventricle.
Vertebra
  One of thirty-three bones of the spinal column.
Vertex
  Crown of the head; topmost point of the vault of the skull.
Vertigo
  Dizziness.
Vitiligo
  Appearance on the skin of white patches of greater or lesser extent, due to simple loss of pigment without other trophic changes.
Volar
  Referring to the palm of the hand.

Z

Zygoma
  Strong bar of bone bridging over the depression of the temple; cheek-bone.

www.ingramcontent.com/pod-product-compliance
Lightning Source LLC
Chambersburg PA
CBHW081820300426
44116CB00014B/2430